WHY L

TRANSFORM YOURSELF

TRANSFORM YOUR ORGANIZATION

MICHAEL MARINO

WHY LEADERS ALWAYS GO FIRST

TRANSFORM YOURSELF

TRANSFORM YOUR ORGANIZATION

Copyright© 2020 by Michael Marino

All rights reserved. No portion of this book may be reproduced, stored in a retrieval system, or transmitted in any form or by any means – electronic, mechanical, photocopy, recording, scanning, or other – except for brief quotations in reviews or articles, without the prior written permission of the publisher.

First Edition

To:
Carol, my wife, my love, my partner in this wonderful life. Thank you for your constant love and encouragement, and for always helping me see the brighter side of life. Love you.

Table of Contents

Introduction 5

Section One: You as the Leader
Chapter One   **A Learner's Mindset** 7
Chapter Two   **The Well-Defined Leader** 15
Chapter Three   **A Leader's Self-Awareness** 26
Chapter Four   **The 5 Traits of Trusted Leadership** 39
Chapter Five   **Role Focus** 47

Section Two: The Leader and Their Team
Chapter Six   **Your Team Leader Role** 52
Chapter Seven   **Your Team Member Role** 60
Chapter Eight   **Strengths-Based Teams** 66
Chapter Nine   **High-Functioning Teams** 77

Section Three: The Leader and Culture
Chapter Ten   **Culture: Purpose, Climate,**
                      and the 6 Key Markers 96
Chapter Eleven   **Exploring Culture** 104
Chapter Twelve   **Designing Culture** 110
Chapter Thirteen   **Building Culture** 114
Chapter Fourteen   **Sustaining Culture** 121

Epilogue: Closing Thoughts 133

References and Suggested Reading 136

Introduction

Transformation can be an intimidating word, and I don't use it often or lightly. It differs from the word "change" in that transformation is thorough and significant; never superficial or partial. "Transformation" is even more intimidating when used in the context of ourselves. Who would want to experience that?

I believe all committed leaders do, and that's why I've created this book—to help committed leaders work through their personal transformation and then be prepared to lead transformation in their organizations.

Ultimately, organizations don't transform, people do. And the good news is the leaders get to go first. From there, transformation can cascade person-by-person, ultimately resulting in organizational transformation. This is important work, which only you can lead. There is no shortcut. It can't be outsourced. It must come from you. I'll paraphrase an expression I read some time ago from an old author: " desire of every leader should e that all that he/s ts done in their people should be truly an ne in themselves."

I've heard it s e that leadership is a verb, and true. I like to s eadership is a "social thing"— words an re used and received. But if it erb, ther nd do we lead? I believe the of the bring out the best in each in ring out the best in the tio his end, **leaders need to bring s first.**

—5—

Since you are reading this book, my true hope is that you are this type of committed leader. I don't know how you got here, but I'm glad that you did. As in a lot of situations in life, I default to the assertion that "people either know enough and want to or hurt enough and have to." Whichever category you fall into doesn't really matter now. Time to move forward.

The pages that follow were written to assist you in your transformational journey. By all means, supplement it as necessary with other content and support yourself with a mentor or coach. Much of what you will embark on will require practice, and that practice can be more effective when we have someone encouraging us and holding us accountable.

I hope you will find that, like some of the best experiences in life, the journey itself will be just as valuable as the final destination. Maybe, just maybe, the journey will never end.

— Your Fellow Journeyer

Section One: You as the Leader

Chapter One
A Learner's Mindset

Since you purchased this book and have now opened to Chapter One, I am working under the assumption that you possess and appreciate, to some degree, a learner's mindset. At the conclusion of your reading, my sincere hope is that you value the concept of a learner's mindset even more.

Entire books and programs have been produced on the subject of mindsets. It is not my intention to reproduce that here. I encourage you to reference the work by Fred Kofman on "Knower vs. Learner" mindsets, as well as Marilee Adam's work on "Judger vs. Learner" mindsets if you want to understand "knowers" and "judger's" better. My goal is to make sure the learner mindset is understood and actively engaged as you start this transformational journey. **The key here is that if you are serious about growth, for you and your organization, then you have to be serious about learning**. It fuels growth. It enables transformation.

Some experts in the field of mindsets have you think of them as distinct and separate, with your ability to deploy one or the other at any time, given the need or situation. Others describe two mindsets on a continuum, shifting from one side to the other. Personally, I enjoy cooking, so I will put mindsets in the context of a "recipe." I believe each one of us has a "mindset recipe" that is part knower, part judger, and part learner. This recipe results in who one is as a person and, ultimately, how you engage as a leader. There are certainly times as leaders when what we know or our ability to judge is important, given the situation at hand, but it should never be the main ingredient. Our desire and ability to learn *should* be. Think of knowing and judging like salt and butter. A small, appropriate amount brings out flavor and adds richness, but too much of either one can take over and ruin an otherwise good experience. I want you to be more liberal with the *learner* mindset, adding a little more and a little more, until it becomes the clear feature of what you are creating.

The initial step in expanding your learner mindset is to simply admit you don't know everything. This is harder for some than for others, especially if we have been told all of our adult lives how "right" we are. And it feels SO GOOD when we fool ourselves into believing we know everything (or just about everything). We feel confident. We feel competent. We are mistake-free and error-free. We have the answer—just ask us. When we dispense our wisdom, our self-esteem rises even higher. It's awesome! It's also perfectly unrealistic and potentially very unhealthy. Rather than focusing on how much we know and becoming a caricature of what we think, the reframe is to consider how much more there is that I can learn. Get energized by things yet to know instead of the known. There is a healthy pinch of humility that is required for this shift. This may make you feel vulnerable and a little uncomfortable. But get used to that feeling, as it's all part of the learner's journey.

The next step after admitting you don't know everything is striving to discover exactly what the things are we don't know that we fooled ourselves into believing we *did* know. What are our true gaps? I have good news and bad news regarding the approach for this. The bad news is, no matter how hard you try, you will never identify these areas through self-reflection and self-assessment. You need the help of others. The good news is, there are always more than enough people around us to help us in this discovery process! It's called feedback, but it's not unlocked without the one key you have in your hand; you have to ask for it. Once unlocked and received, it must be cherished and never wasted. If you don't currently have trusted, wise people speaking into your life and helping you learn, you are at a great disadvantage. I encourage you to get this support in place immediately. But remember, once received, it must be cherished. Don't ever let it go to waste.

This reminds me of a time years ago when I worked with a Fortune 100 company filled with bright, ambitious people. Our senior vice-president had his immediate team go through a 360-degree feedback process and scheduled a full day offsite for us to share findings and learn from the experience (we'll get into the reasons as to why this probably wasn't the best idea when we get in the Teams section later ☺). Our SVP decided he would lead by example and share the feedback he received first, with the goal of engaging the team in a transparent discussion of the feedback. He proceeded to share the findings in his report, which, to no one's surprise, were not terribly positive. By the time he got to the end of the report, you could tell he was getting quite uncomfortable and was attempting to use humor to offset his uneasiness. This is when he announced that he knew himself so well that his feedback results couldn't possibly be accurate. In seconds, he both threw away any chance for learning and dismissed the input from his team as useless. To make matters worse, he decided that instead of using the day for the 360-degree exercise, we would instead do goal setting for the next fiscal year. So now everyone else lost the opportunity to learn as well—all because one individual struggled to acknowledge he didn't know everything.

The last step in this process we'll cover is what to do with the feedback we get. In short, USE IT! By this I mean embrace the feedback; see this as an opportunity to learn, to grow, to improve ... to transform. Be open about it. You may want to engage a professional coach to assist you in this process—someone who can support, encourage, and hold you accountable. Or work with a mentor you have access to. But just like we need others to provide some of the inputs to our learning and transformation, we also need others so we can grow and develop along the journey. As uncomfortable as it may seem, transformation is a team sport.

Next, I want us to spend some time on two different types of learning because the remainder of this book is pretty much segmented by them. They are vertical learning and horizontal learning. The field of psychology tends to describe vertical learning as the development of "who we are", while horizontal learning is more about "what we know and do." This distinction will serve just fine as we proceed on our journey.

Section 1 of this book, "You as The Leader", focuses almost entirely on vertical learning or development. It will be personal. Things like meaning, purpose, and principles will be covered. Becoming more self-aware will be addressed. This will become the basis, and the beginning, of your personal transformation. I say "basis" as it will serve as the foundation on which all else will be built. I say "beginning" because vertical learning tends to be the most challenging type of learning and will require a long-term perspective. It takes time. It evolves. It's a process in which the value lies as much in the journey itself as it is the destination. So please be patient and committed.

Sections 2 and 3, "The Leader and Your Team" and "The Leader and Culture", will focus more on horizontal learning or development. They will include using capabilities and capacity as a leader to bring about transformation in your organization. But remember what was said in the introduction—organizations don't transform, people do. When we talk about transforming your organization, we mean the impact you have on the people in it that can, in turn, bring about overall organization transformation.

That final thing I want to challenge leaders about learning is having the courage to be an "Unlearner." We need to get rid of some of the thinking we have stored away. I'm talking about old habits, misconceptions, outdated information, etc. You know, the stuff that is hard to let go of. Think of it like that old article of clothing you pull out on Saturday mornings. The one your spouse has tried to hide and even bought a replacement for; something much, much better. But you still look for it and throw it on every Saturday morning. Why? Because you know it so well. It's comfortable, familiar. It's easy to slip on. It feels good. You feel attached to it.

But right next to it is the article your spouse gave you to replace it. It's new and improved. Easier to take care of. A little warmer, perhaps. Probably fits and looks better. But we hesitate to make the switch. Will it be as comfortable? As easy to wear? Will I feel different with it on? It will be OK, I promise. Give it a few tries. Wow, it does feel pretty good! It *is* a bit warmer. Even smells a little better. Think I'll just move that old one to the back of the closet. Better yet, I'll donate it. But wait, it really isn't worth keeping or donating. It's pretty worn out. I think it's best to just throw it away at this point.

That's the whole idea with unlearning. In order to embrace what is new, better, and smarter we need to let go of those things we've gotten comfortable with that are no longer of good use. We can't stay the same, and that means some things need to be rotating in and out. We need to break the pattern. Sometimes it's easier to have someone help us identify these things for us — ideally, someone close to us and someone we trust.

I'll wrap up this section on a learner's mindset with a story about a company I ran across recently. The CEO clearly has a learner's mindset and wanted to encourage it throughout her organization. She wanted to create a culture of learning and continuous improvement. How did she create this culture? She developed a program that promoted reading by paying employees $10 for every non-fiction book they read. Each book is posted on the company website, including the reader's insights and lessons learned from reading the book. Thousands of books have been read and shared, and tens of thousands of dollars have been paid to the employees who have read them. In addition, they also donate books to jails, prisons, schools, churches, mentoring programs, and non-profit organizations. To date, they have donated over one million books! That's developing a learning culture in your organization and impacting the community at the same time. Awesome!

Chapter Two
The Well-Defined Leader

The challenge throughout this book will be that leaders focus first on their own transformation before attempting to transform their organizations. Specifically, in this chapter the challenge is to focus first on your own existence, your own presence, and your own integrity before moving on to inspire and motivate others. Be real with yourself so that you can be real with others. Some have never begun this type of journey while others may have traveled the path for some time. That's OK. Wherever you are on this journey of self-discovery, the intentional focus will provide dividends.

Let's start with a snapshot of what is meant by "Well-Defined." A leader that is well-defined has a deep understanding of themselves, is self-differentiated, is non-anxious, is persistent and consistent; all while willing to be open and vulnerable. Know any leaders like this? Probably not, as they are becoming extinct day by day. Despite the overwhelming amount of content and programs available on leadership development, the counterbalance (consisting of too little time, too much pressure for profit, impatient shareholders and stakeholders, and the rest) has turned most leaders into transaction-based, short-term-focused, conflict-avoiding managers of activities. Did we start out with that end in mind? Of course not. So how come so many of us end up there? I submit it is because we were never well-defined to begin with, or that definition got lost somewhere along the way. Regardless of the reason, now is the time to get well-defined. But how does one do that?

We will cover two core elements for any well-defined leader: Purpose and Principles. I believe each one of us is uniquely made and for a unique purpose—your North Star, if you will. Once that purpose is understood, then we must possess individual principles that guide how we will fulfill it. As simple as this sounds, and as clear it will seem from the other side, there can be a fair amount of heavy lifting involved in getting there.

Unique Purpose
To be clear, when I say "your unique purpose" I am not referring to just your work purpose, per se. I'm talking about your *life* purpose. I'm talking existential. What is the purpose of my very existence? If you've pondered this question before, good for you. If not, and it feels a bit too existential for you, hang in there. It will be worth it. Then we can tie back to how it plays out in organizational life.

First, I need to offer a framework for context here. The framework consists of a "Why", a "What", and a "How." While it's important for all three components to be defined, they do not necessarily have to follow a particular order in their development. Now, there has been a fair amount already written in this area, and it's not my intention to contradict what exists, but to simplify. Everyone knows that Simon Sinek wrote the book on "Why", literally, and he implores us to start with "Why." My struggle with that is twofold. First, he and other experts in the field still mix the terms "why" and "purpose," which I believe creates some confusion. Second, while I think it is great to start with "Why", it's equally as effective to work back to the "Why" for some people. I offer the following outline for my "Why", "What", and "How" framework.

- **Why** – the combined set of experiences, beliefs, knowledge, and causes that serves as the source of our unique purpose. It can be items we value and want to carry forward or negative experiences we vow to overcome. It can be things that actually occurred or the lack thereof.
- **What (Purpose)** – because of the impact of the "Why", this is what I believe is the reason for my existence. This is what I was made/shaped to do. It brings energy to our lives—not drains them. It's why we rise each morning. **This is our purpose.**
- **How** – this is where my "What" meets other people; the way in which it is lived out. It may look differently at home than it does at work, but

it is always an interpretation of your unique purpose.

The reason I say the sequence of discovery can vary is that some of you are living into your purpose, or "What", already, without consciously going through the "Why" discovery. Your "Why" subconsciously informed your "What" along the way, providing passion and energy without you necessarily being self-aware of the cause/effect nature. In your case, I recommend spending time in discovering and understanding your "Why" fully and then confirm, modify, or, if necessary, restate your purpose. Sinek and others have done a wonderful job of identifying the types of questions to lead you through discovering your "Why", and I encourage you to spend ample time there. But my goal is not to rehash how to discover your "Why." Instead, my goal is to establish the importance of understanding these things in order to be transformed into a Well-Defined Leader.

Let me share my personal purpose with you as an example.

- **Why** – I've seen what happens to people when they lose hope and think things will never get better; the personal suffering that takes place as individuals feel that there is nothing they or anyone else can do to make the situation better.

They are ready to give up. Life for them no longer has meaning or potential. This grieves my heart.
- **What (Purpose)** – My purpose is to be a bridge, a bridge of hope; helping others in any way possible get from where they are to where they want to be.
- **How** – Coaching, mentoring, advising, and developing individuals and teams.

Here is one more example. I think Christians and non-Christians alike are all familiar with the most popular verse in the bible: John 3:16. It goes like this: "For God so loved the world that he gave his one and only son, that whoever believes in him shall not perish, but have eternal life." Let's break that out using our framework to understand God's purpose in this.

- **Why** – Because God so loves the world
- **What (Purpose)** – That people not perish but have eternal life
- **How** – He gave His one and only son

Hopefully, these examples are helpful. I'm convinced that a leader will have their greatest impact when they fully know who they are and why they do what they do. I'm also convinced, through thirty-plus years of personal success and failure, as well as professional observation, that this does not come easily to most leaders. Or anyone for that matter. I encourage you to be intentional about developing your purpose. Don't be afraid if it doesn't snap into place right away. For some it will. For others, it could take months or even years. Personally, mine has slowly but surely evolved over the course of a decade. Time helps us fine-tune it.

To help you arrive at your unique purpose, consider asking yourself questions along the lines of the following:

- What are you doing when you lose track of time and the world around you?
- What would you spend your time doing if money were no object?
- What pulls on your heart when you see or hear about it?
- What do others say you are incredibly gifted at?
- What do you and your best friend talk about most?
- What is the theme of your favorite movie?
- Where do you find your mind going when you have idle time?
- What experiences from childhood made the greatest impression on you?
- What have you accomplished that brings you the most joy?
- What things do people come to you for?

Take your time and work through these questions. Look for the common themes in the answers. The more time you spend on this, the clearer your purpose will become. If you get stuck, feel free to share the questions and responses with another trusted person. They may see the themes and connections better than you can yourself.

I'll wrap up this section on purpose with a quote. It comes from a man by the name of Norm Sonju, who was co-founder and former General Manager of the Dallas Mavericks professional basketball team. When looking back on his career, he said, "When you're a leader, it's so important before you lead, that you know who you are." A truer statement has never been spoken. Unfortunately, many of us are thrust into leadership roles before we have figured out exactly "who we are." Our western culture focuses more on what we do than who we are, sadly. But it's never too late to engage this journey. We'll be better leaders for it.

Individual Principles

While I prefer the term "principle" over "values" or "core values", I don't want this to be a sticking point that causes one to miss the bigger message. So, if you prefer "core values", feel free to substitute when you read the word "principle."

The reason I prefer "principle" is based on my own understanding that our principles are what define us and declare what others can expect from us. Principles should represent how we behave and interact with others. It's more about actions as compared to values, which tend to represent what we *believe*. But again, this is not the main point.

The main point is that in combination with your Unique Purpose your Individual Principles should differentiate you from everyone else. As mentioned, I personally believe that each one of us is uniquely made for a unique purpose, and to help us achieve that purpose we have our unique, individual principles. Developing these principles can be both a paradigm-shifting and liberating experience. Principles are the underpinnings of each individual—the foundations for our behavior and our standards of conduct regardless of the situation or vocation. They are not up for debate or compromise. They tend to be unchanging. They represent how we want others to see and experience us.

When I coach individuals, my recommendation is that they focus on three to five clear, concise principles. The framework requires that each principle be stated as a one-word noun. Each principle then gets a written description. I want to be clear here—a description, not a definition. More of what it looks like than what it is. Then I ask them to provide a shortlist of both mindset examples and observable behaviors that correspond to each principle. Below is an example from a past client.

Principle: Courage

Description: Overcoming challenges, barriers, and anxiety while speaking and acting with honesty and integrity

Mindset: Believe that conflict can be healthy
Be open to thoughts, ideas, and opinions of others
Have resolve, with humility
Be free from fear
Keep the unique purpose first in mind

Behaviors: Willing to engage in healthy conflict
Willing to take risks
Seeking to push through fear and be open and vulnerable
Willing to lean in and be fully present

The last part of the exercise is to create a few evaluation questions for yourself—questions you can routinely ask yourself to assess whether your behaviors are congruent with the principles. Examples could be "Have I engaged or skirted around conflict?", or "Have I taken a risk or played it safe?" As a coach, I revisit these with my clients on a regular basis and encourage them to do the same on their own, giving a grade each time. And now that you have a "learner's mindset", I recommend you also ask those around you to assess your alignment with the principles as well. The goal is to see steady improvement over time. If you are not seeing progress, you will have to spend some time assessing why that is. You may need to remove something from your life. You may want to get help in the form of accountability if a principle is important to you. Or you may need to be honest and decide that although it sounded good, it's just not a life principle for you. That's OK too.

The existence of a clearly understood Unique Purpose and strong Individual Principles is the foundation for becoming a Well-Defined Leader. Armed with this, leaders will more consistently demonstrate the following:

- The capacity to get outside of the emotional climate of the day
- Persistence in the face of resistance, and even rejection
- A non-anxious, while at times challenging, presence
- Remaining consciously responsive vs. emotionally reactive
- Being comfortable with other's discomfort/displeasure
- Determined, objective decision making

Not only will you experience greater meaning in your life and work, but you will also now be positioned to bring greater meaning to your organization. We'll talk about how that plays out when we get to "The Leader and Culture" section. For now, you can expect to experience fewer peaks and valleys. You will feel less stress and anxiety because you have a clearer picture of exactly who you are. Outside stimuli won't have the same effect on you. You will be more comfortable making decisions and taking calculated risks. All because you are better grounded in your purpose and principles.

Chapter Three
A Leader's Self-Awareness

Much has been written in the last half-century on the topic of self-awareness. My goal is not to go into the deep psychology or philosophy on the subject, but to simply provide a couple of aspects of self-awareness that will be of primary benefit to all leaders. To this end, I'll frame the discussion around a basic description of self-awareness as **"one's ability to understand where they are both emotionally and physically at any particular moment."** To stop and tune into your mind and body—this is important for our own health and well-being, of course, but also for the "health" of whatever system we may be operating in. By system I mean your family, your workplace, your circle of friends—all are systems that we participate in.

The two aspects of self-awareness I want to focus on are what I'm calling "Red Zone/Blue Zone Location" and "Mirror and Window."

Red Zone/Blue Zone Location
For this topic, I admittedly will borrow and take privilege with the fine work of my dear friends Joe Jurkowski and Jim Osterhaus, who penned the book titled *Red Zone Blue Zone – Turning Conflict into Opportunity*. They do a tremendous job of identifying triggers of our own internal conflict and how that is

experienced in conflicted exchanges with others. My focus is primarily around utilizing the Red Zone/Blue Zone concept to help you easily locate yourself at any given time, based on what you are thinking and feeling.

The first step in this self-awareness is to stop for a moment. Call a time-out for yourself. I realize this is not the easiest task when you are in the middle of a critical conversation or animated discussion, but if we are feeling a sense of stress and/or anxiety, we need to hit the pause button on whatever we are engaged in. Take a deep breath, recalibrate yourself, excuse yourself from the room for a moment—whatever it requires.

The next step is what is referred to as "locating yourself." My version of this is to quickly assess whether you currently reside in the Red Zone or Blue Zone. To help locate yourself, below are examples of how you are thinking and feeling in each.

RED ZONE	BLUE ZONE
Focused on self	Focused on the priority
Closed-off	Open-minded
Defensive	Curious
Opinionated	Listening
Threatened	Trusting
Prideful	Humble

We all tend to spend more of our time in the Red Zone than the Blue Zone, so don't beat yourself up. In fact, we are programmed this way. We have a survival instinct that kicks in automatically, where we tend to go into our self-protect mode. We just need to be extra diligent in our self-awareness so that we locate ourselves and shift towards the Blue Zone as quickly as possible. The key here is not to dwell in the Red Zone when we, sadly, find ourselves located here, but simply recognize it, then release it. Don't get stuck there. Forgive yourself and put your energy into shifting.

Shifting can prove difficult, for sure, but with practice, we all get better at it. It's difficult because the triggers that put us in the Red Zone in the first place are very strong and very real. These triggers include wanting to be seen as competent, not being in control, experiencing a perceived lack of appreciation or respect, and, lastly, our very survival. Again, the key is to recognize what triggers are at play and then release them. One way to release them, and the feelings associated with them, is to reframe our thinking. For example, if we could take a deep breath for a moment, we might see that rather than people challenging us for control, they might just have a high degree of ownership and responsibility. Maybe it's not about me at all, but I got triggered to feel that way. Embrace this and start shifting over to the Blue Zone. Instead of others challenging your competency, the reframe may be that they too want to make meaningful contributions because they are committed to making a difference. The use of a reframe will be your best tool in moving from Red Zone to Blue Zone, but it will take commitment and practice. A good starting point is to play back recent episodes of Red Zone behavior. Write down what the situation was and how you reacted. Note what triggered you to go Red Zone. Then spend time reframing the scenario and journal how you would have handled it differently. This will make it easier when you encounter the next live situation.

Remember, whenever you are in a situation and it feels a bit stressed or there seems to be a disproportionate amount of energy in the room, take a quick mental break to locate yourself. From that point, you will be able to consciously respond to the situation and be less led to react from an emotion-driven standpoint.

"Mirror and Window"
It happens all the time. The owner/operator of his or her business, or the executive team of the typical organization, starts down the same thought process. Performance just isn't what it should be. Things seem "stuck." We're not growing as we have historically grown. We're not realizing our full potential. Whatever the description used is, the conclusion is pretty much always the same—"Something needs to change."

This typically leads to an exercise of finding fault by function—looking for the easy answer. Marketing isn't generating enough opportunities. Sales isn't closing deals at the rate they should be. Human Resources isn't providing the right people or training. Operations has become less efficient. Finance needs to restructure pricing. You get the picture—there are plenty of targets and more than enough darts to make this an all-day exercise. Especially when those darts land close to one of the participant's areas of responsibility; when pride and emotion enter the fray. Now there is no shortage of energy in the room—but hit the pause button on this scenario for a moment.

A *slightly* more enlightened approach may lead to a discussion of more foundational issues. The word "culture" will probably come up. Maybe a reference to a "systemic problem." Possibly, the concept of an "adaptive issue" might be voiced. Or the need for more teamwork. Now we are into topics that can go on for a day or more but addressing them will almost certainly require outside help from a consulting expert. Who knows, maybe this gets labeled a "strategic initiative" for focus in the upcoming fiscal year. I'm not making this stuff up. I've been part of these exercises, and if you are being honest, so have you.

Both of these scenarios could very well provide *some* insight into the performance issues and ways in which to improve. At the same time, both scenarios have one blinding thing in common. Do you see it? Whether we are attempting to find fault by function or identifying possible foundational issues, the perspective was the same. From where we sit, we are looking out at all the possibilities around us. How often do we turn our perspective inward and truly start by asking what we may be contributing to the issues? This reflection is the second aspect of self-awareness we'll get into.

I call this the "mirror and window" dynamic. The vast majority of the time, our first response is to "look through the window" in trying to identify what's not working. The problem must be "out there" somewhere, and it's our job to identify and fix it, right? This is akin to someone who goes to the dentist, is told they have a couple of cavities, and decides it's caused by everything from the amount sweeteners in foods today to the effectiveness of their toothbrush and toothpaste. It couldn't possibly have to do with my diet choices and dental hygiene practices, could it?

This is where the mirror comes in. As a general rule of thumb – and this applies to work, marriage, you name it – **one should always pick up the mirror before peering through the window.** Sounds simple, I know. Mirror first, then the window … I get it. But if it is that simple, then why don't we do it consistently? Ask yourself that question and force yourself to answer it. Write it down on the opposite side of the notepaper or phone app note that says "mirror first, then window." Keep it handy as a reminder. I know, it's so much easier to find or assign blame elsewhere, and that might actually work for a short period of time. But sooner or later, the mirror must come out—if you are serious about solving the problem and if you are serious about being an effective leader. And since you are reading this book, I have to assume the answer to both challenges is a resounding "Yes."

Personally speaking, I have very rarely bumped into a problem that I have not contributed to in some form or fashion. Let me say that again: I have very rarely bumped into a problem that I have not contributed to in some form or fashion. How about you? So, the first step is to simply remember that there is a legitimate chance that I'm partially at fault for the issue we're trying to solve. If this ends up being the only thing you take away from this book, I'm quite OK with that. It's that important.

From there, take a good, long stare into your mirror. Ask yourself what you may have contributed to the problem you are facing. It may be something tangible or intangible. It could be something you did or something you failed to do; maybe even a combination of both. If you're not sure or clear on it, here's a crazy idea: ask someone. Did I in some way contribute to the issue we are now faced with? How so? Can you give me an example? You may be surprised by what you hear.

A Leader's Self-Awareness

At this point, you can put your mirror down. You've told yourself and/or heard from others what your potential contributions are. Now it's time to own your stuff. Don't rationalize it. Refrain from blame-shifting. Try not to tell yourself stories to feel better about it. But no peeking out the window yet. No one else is going to jump in and own their role in the problem until you lead the way. Because you're the leader, and leaders always go first.

I want to stop here for a minute and deal with what I'm guessing may be a bit of resistance on your part. And resistance is OK. It's part of the process and, in the end, a great teacher. But before we get into the types of possible resistance, let's get on the same page regarding one key fact. And that fact is that you are either "the" or "a" leader right now. So, we need to speak to possible resistance within this context.

Let's start with the easiest form of resistance to deal with—denial. After looking in the mirror and asking others, you've reached the certain conclusion that you contributed exactly nothing to the issue or problem at hand. You are innocent. In the most respectful and Christian-like way possible, may I say it's quite likely you are telling yourself a story you want to hear. Remember, it could be something done or not done, said or not said, or maybe even the way it was said or done. So, give yourself some credit because chances are you need to own something in the process. I encourage you to spend a little more time with the mirror or ask another person or two. Trust me, you'll uncover something!

The next type of resistance is one of comparison: I'll own my stuff but there is a lot more that others need to own. This could be true, but let's talk about these "others." Are they in over their heads? In the wrong role? Without the necessary capabilities? Not trained or developed effectively? Is it a vendor not performing up to par? A problematic client? Did they lack context or understanding? Did they make a poor decision? Is their behavior an issue? Their attitude? I could go on, but I'd rather go back to the key fact established earlier; you are either "the" or "a" leader. If that is true, then let's revisit some of the questions above, with a slight twist. Who should know if someone is in over their heads? Who would know if someone is in the wrong role? Who hired someone that is not capable of fulfilling their position? Who was responsible for their training and development? Who selected or signed-off on the vendor? Who decided to take on a problematic client? Who was aware of a poor decision being made? Yep, that would be us, the leaders. I don't make this point in an attempt to assign all blame to the leaders but, through comparison, to simply remind us that the decisions we make can indirectly contribute to issues each and every day. It comes with the territory. But sometimes this can be a blind spot for us.

There is at least one other area of resistance I'm guessing may be in play. If you have been a leader for a significant period of time and/or you possibly come from an industry or background of command and control leadership, you may be thinking that this "owning my stuff" approach may have you come across as a weak leader. We'll talk about this more in the chapter about The Leader and Their Team, but if you want to be an effective leader, trust is critical. Our organizations want to trust their leadership. And, as you know, trust takes time to develop but can be lost in an instant. Being a leader with character and integrity is the most effective way of earning trust. By being self-aware, recognizing your contributions to problems, and owning your role in them demonstrates your character and integrity. People want honesty, transparency, and, yes, even vulnerability from their leadership. Using your mirror and owning your stuff makes you a stronger leader, not a weaker one.

Let's face it, whether it is good or bad, our organizations tend to be a reflection of us as leaders. They take on our personalities, our behaviors, and even our language. We'll cover more of this when discussing The Leader and Culture, but it certainly applies here. If we don't want an organization that makes excuses and looks for ways to blame-shift, then we have to model those principles and behaviors consistently. I'm going to use this next phrase throughout this book because it's so true. **Leadership is a social thing.** People are ALWAYS watching and observing. Our actions and words ALWAYS have an impact.

This reminds me of a consulting project I was part of with one of my previous firms. An organization came to us requesting we provide some assessment/discovery work. They were preparing to embark on a new vision and wanted to take the pulse of the organization to see if the timing was right. Now, our firm took our discovery work very seriously, to the point that we would regularly tell clients that they were indeed not ready to make a major move. We believed that providing that truth was the best service we could provide when it was appropriate. And this client knew, going into the discovery work, exactly how we operated, so they knew what they were getting. After our initial meetings with leadership, we had concerns as to whether they were the type of leaders that would be willing to take some of the discovery findings and "pull out their mirror." But we decided to proceed despite our reservations. We fielded an organization-wide survey, facilitated numerous focus groups, and conducted a handful of one-on-one interviews with leadership. As we summarized the findings, there were multiple themes regarding the leadership's effectiveness that signaled the organization was not ready for a major move at that time. There were some key leadership and cultural issues that would need to be addressed prior to any changes.

Well, we shared the findings with leadership, highlighting a handful of critical items and why we believed it would be in their best interest to not proceed until devoting time to address them. As part of our effort, we respectfully challenged them to take the feedback to heart and, rather than rationalize or dismiss it, try to understand how they may be contributing to the issues that were expressed. Said another way, we were asking them to spend some time in the mirror. But the more we tried to slide the mirror their way, the more they preferred to look through the window. You can probably guess what we heard.

"That's not accurate."

"That was years ago. Things have changed."

"I know who would have said that. Let me tell you why they are wrong."

"They just don't understand what we are trying to do."

"That happened just one time."

The rationalizations, the denials, the haste to create an alternative narrative were all happening before our very eyes. In a last gasp effort to get somebody, anybody, to even consider peeking into the mirror, I offered this plea. Could there possibly be one, just one, theme identified that might have merit and be worthy of leadership taking it to heart? Any one—pick one. Their response? You guessed it—they didn't believe any of the findings were accurate and were committed to plowing ahead. We provided our final thoughts, thanked them for the opportunity, and concluded the meeting. Afterward, we decided, as we would on occasion when faced with this type of situation, that we would not move onto the next phase of work with this client. It probably won't surprise you that, based on our interactions at the finish of the discovery phase, they came to the same conclusion!

Chapter Four
The 5 Traits of Trusted Leadership

Trust takes years to build, seconds to break, and forever to repair. We've all heard this or something like it. I like to say that building trust works like a dimmer switch, but breaking trust works like an on/off switch being switched instantly to off. For all the talk about the importance of trust, it seems leaders today still underestimate the amount of work it takes to build it. Maybe it's a function of limited time, maybe limited knowledge. But without trust, we cannot effectively lead. Trust is the basis for leadership, the foundation. Below is what I suggest you consider if you are genuinely interested in building trust. It's called the 5 Traits of Trusted Leadership, and, to keep it simple, each trait begins with the letter "C".

At the core of trusted leadership, and essential in building trust, is **"Care"**. Caring is a simple concept that we are all familiar with, but far too few of us truly demonstrate. The old saying goes, "They won't care what you know until they know that you care." How true! Caring means you are committed to investing time in your people, getting to know them – what's important to them, their goals and aspirations, their interests and passions – and what makes them unique. All individuals have an innate desire to belong, contribute, and make a difference. The care they

—39—

experience from you provides them this sense of belonging and leads to them contributing their unique talents and strengths to the shared goals. Care cannot be faked, so before trying it, look inwardly as to why you are doing it. Be genuine. Be authentic. The only thing worse than no care at all is care that is insincere.

Without care in place, your words will fall on deaf ears. Worse yet, they may sound like monotonous noises that get ignored at first, but then become irritating. This reminds me of a bible verse that is connected to a very familiar passage we have all heard at wedding ceremonies. We have all heard the words from what's called the Love Chapter, spoken over a soon-to-be-married couple: "Love is patient, love is kind. It does not envy, it does not boast, it is not proud. It does not dishonor others, it is not self-seeking, it is not easily angered, it keeps no record of wrongs." Sounds remarkably familiar, right? What probably isn't as familiar, because it tends not to be included, is the verse that opens that chapter. To paraphrase for our purposes, it says "I can have all the gifts and talents in the world, but if I don't have love, I am only a resounding gong or a clanging cymbal." Translation of the Greek word used for "love" in this verse means "selfless concern for the welfare of others." Let's use that definition for care. If our people don't believe we have a selfless concern for their well-being, our words will sound like resounding gongs and clanging cymbals to them. Let's not be gongs and cymbals!

The next trait is **"Character."** People want to follow high-character leaders—individuals who operate from a position of integrity. At the very minimum, leaders should be committed to principles of honesty and morality. This gets at our individual principles discussed in a previous chapter. If you don't have yours locked in and described, now is the time to do so. Capture them, share them, and, most importantly, live them. Be willing and able to "walk the talk." I referred to this type of leader as a "well-defined leader." They know what they are about and these core principles guide all they do and how they do it. After all, leadership is a "social thing", meaning people are always observing our words and actions, and they are looking for high-character leaders to trust in and follow.

As important as it is to consistently "walk-the-talk" when it comes to our character, it is equally as important to be honest and transparent when we stumble. If we've acted in a way that is incongruent with our principles, or we've made a decision that lacks integrity, we need to be able to own it. Whether we recognize it or it gets brought to our attention, we must call it what it is, own it, and commit to being better. People will respect you for taking this approach, building greater trust going forward.

The final element of a leader's character has to do with dependability. Does the leader follow through on what they say will be done? Can the leader be counted on to come through when needed? Dependability is a building block in developing and maintaining trust. Being dependable tells others that they matter. This is a perfect place to lead by example. If people determine that they cannot depend on you, then you will not be able to depend on them.

The third trait is **"Communication"**. Two-way communication. Remember that leadership is a "social thing" and strong communication is a must. Let's start with inbound communication. How good a listener would you say you are? Do you listen to learn, or do you listen to respond? There is a big difference. One way to assess this is to watch how much time you leave between when someone stops talking to you and when you launch into your response. If there is little or no air time, chances are you are not fulling listening. Active listening includes giving someone your undivided attention, listening for understanding, asking open-ended questions, clarifying what we think we heard, and confirming before moving on.

This requires a very intentional focus and a genuine interest in what the other person is saying. It also takes practice. Get good at asking open-ended questions and view people's responses as possible avenues to ask additional questions/pursue further. Allow them time to enrich their responses with personal stories and examples. Watch for facial expressions and body language to help guide you. When they're done, and if it's appropriate, thank them for sharing their thoughts. Tell them why it was helpful to you. In our "get to the bottom line" world I realize this is a significant mind-shift, but if you are committed to building trust with your communication, it will be well worth it.

Regarding our outbound communication, the most important aspect is to be intentional. Whether it's one-on-one conversations, team meetings, or organizational communiques, leaders must be planful in their efforts. Each interaction is either building trust … or eroding it. Don't waste any of it. That being said, it's also vitally important for leaders to be open and available for impromptu connections. Our people need these interactions, and they need us to be present in them. Don't worry about what you had scheduled or what you might be late for. Instead, turn your full attention to the interaction at hand. Lastly, if the goal of your communication is to generate a commitment of action by others, please be very specific as to <u>what</u> is expected, <u>when</u> it is expected, and in <u>what form</u> or medium. For example, "Can I expect that you will have the report completed by Friday, saved as a PDF, and emailed to the team by end of day?" The biggest breakdown in communication is due to a lack of specificity. If we are doing the asking, then the onus is on us to provide the specifics. If people are asking for greater specificity, they aren't doing it to frustrate you or complicate matters — they just want to make sure they deliver what you are expecting. This is a good thing. As your communication improves, so will your organization's trust in you.

The fourth trait is **"Capacity."** Our capacity to lead is directly correlated to our capacity to learn. Do you consider yourself a "learner"; someone on a life-long journey to expand and improve? Or do you see yourself as one who already "knows" all that is necessary and believes they have all the answers? Be honest. Our organizations can only grow if we are growing as leaders, plain and simple. If you sense your organization is stuck or in maintenance mode, it probably is because you are as well. Whether we like it or not, organizations are merely a reflection of their leadership. To begin, every leader should have an acute awareness of their natural talents and strengths, as these are what we naturally lead from. I recommend starting with a simple self-assessment. There are several useful tools that exist today, and you may have already utilized one or more of them. My recommendation is Gallup's StrengthsFinder. This assessment not only identifies your natural talents and helps you understand how they can be leveraged to make you a unique leader, but it also creates awareness of how others may experience you due to the expression of your talents.

We'll go deeper on strengths in the section The Leader and Their Team. With this foundational understanding, your learning journey can then continue as you expand and improve skills in other areas, based on your business model and organization's needs.

For every leader, the capacity to learn has to cover, at a minimum, three vital areas: 1) crafting and communicating vision, 2) building strong teams, and 3) developing a thriving culture. If you are not investing time in these areas with a "Learner's Mindset", you are doing your organization a disservice. These are fundamental to a healthy, thriving organization, and we'll devote time to them in later chapters. Remember, as your organization observes your commitment to personal growth and capacity, its trust in you as a leader will grow as well.

The fifth and final trait, and the one that applies to all the other traits, is **"Consistency."** To be a trusted leader, the principles outlined here need to be demonstrated both intentionally and regularly. All of them! We need to be committed and stay committed. Not only will people notice the improved approach and effort, but they will also notice if you fall back on old behaviors. They will help you stay on point, staying committed. None of us will be great all 5 Traits, but the key is to pursue each of them to the best of our ability. Our effort makes the difference! It will take practice, probably with missteps along the way to learn from, but it will be oh so worth it! I apologize in advance, but let's use a baseball analogy. In baseball, they refer to a "5 Tool" player as one that has speed and power, hits for average, fields well, and possesses a strong throwing arm. The rare player that excels in all five will most likely find their way into the Hall of Fame. The other 99% of players make efforts in all five areas, striving to improve, enabling them to have successful careers. You don't have to be a Hall of Fame Leader to earn the trust and respect of your organization. Just make the commitment to be a "major leaguer!"

As we set out at the beginning, building trust is work. It takes time. It takes commitment. But to be an effective leader, trust is essential. With our words and actions, we are constantly either building it up or breaking it down. Never assume it's always there, and never take it for granted. If for some reason you break it, get to work at repairing it immediately. You'll be a better leader for it.

Chapter Five
Role Focus

I want to get into one final topic on You as the Leader, and although it is quite simple conceptually, it tends to be quite difficult in application. It is the topic of role and responsibilities.

You and I have seen it happen, I'm sure. It could be an individual who gets promoted into a leadership role based on a strong track record of performance, or an entrepreneur whose role shifts from start-up to grow and sustain. What we see is that how they function in the new role may not change from how they functioned in the prior roles.

One of my past firms had a large federal government agency as a long-term client. A problem we would always run into was that directors and vice presidents, when promoted into position, still operated like the frontline managers they once were. They were really good frontline managers; that's what got them promoted. But that was not what was required in their new role. The more they operated as they did in the past, the more they undermined the effectiveness and engagement of their own team. Trust and accountability went out the window, while conflict filled the room. Unfortunately, we never had the opportunity to work with these leaders BEFORE they were in position, only AFTER they were promoted and the problems started.

The thing I want to focus on is how leaders see or define their roles. My recommendation is to define it as, "What is my primary function organizationally?" This primary function will change drastically as you move up in any organization, as will the tasks and responsibilities associated with it. With each role, we need to define the primary function AND the responsibilities needed to fulfill that function. Easy, right?

Back to my federal agency example. A frontline manager's primary function may be to ensure flawless daily operations. Their responsibilities could include hiring and onboarding team members, managing schedules, dealing with customer issues, daily reporting, etc. All these tasks are required in order to fulfill their primary function of ensuring flawless daily operations.

The director or vice president of this agency has a quite different primary function as its leader. It would involve communicating a vision and objectives for the agency, and ensuring the team is properly aligned and resourced to execute with success. The responsibilities of the leader include establishing the culture, developing the teams, holding people accountable, communicating effectively—all focused on the performance of their direct reports/teams to maintain a healthy climate or environment for exceptional performance.

Based on the differences in primary function and responsibilities, you can see the trouble that emerges when a leader is still trying to fulfill the function and take on the responsibilities of their managers. And oh, by the way, this works in the other direction as well.

Trouble also occurs when the managers think their function and responsibilities are those of the director. Everyone needs to understand their primary function and responsibilities and, for the sake of what is best for the organization, stay in their space. Especially the leaders. In their case, they have the potential of not only causing disfunction in their current work team but, because "leadership is a social thing", their words and actions are observed and repeated by others as they become leaders. The disfunction is carried forward, unfortunately, until someone breaks the chain through their own learning and development. Please stop and think about your current role and whether you are taking on the role and responsibilities of your subordinates. Be honest. If you are, please give back the work ASAP, and stay 100% focused on your role as the leader.

Related to this issue, and more prevalent in founder-led organizations and/or small companies, is the problem of a leader having too many primary functions. Said another way, leaders trying to wear too many hats. I have personally made this mistake in the past, and I have been part of founder-led organizations where I've seen it at play.

For me, I spent ten years as the managing partner of a boutique consulting firm. It was a small firm, with as few as 10 employees at one point and as many as 30 when in growth mode. I found myself in the following roles, at the same time:

- Partner/Owner – with other partners crafting vision, strategy, objectives, culture, etc.
- COO – handling daily, weekly, monthly operations
- CFO – ensuring financial viability and overseeing performance
- CPO – people-related issues, performance management, benefits, etc.
- Sales and Marketing – doing business development, overseeing marketing and promotion
- Consultant – delivering services to key clients

Do you think all these hats made it easy to remember what my primary function was? Do you think my leadership was effective and consistent? Of course not. Ramifications? I suffered, but, more importantly, the organization suffered. The lack of effective and consistent leadership directly impacted the engagement level of the team. They weren't sure exactly where we were heading, or how we were going to get there. Holding people accountable was challenging at best. Decision making was slow, frustrating the team and our clients. Our execution suffered. It was not the most joyful place to work. People left the firm, in part, because I was wearing too many hats and trying to play too many roles.

It's virtually impossible to stay focused on your primary function as a leader when wearing too many hats. It's not fair to you or the organization. But how do we get in this position? Is it out of sheer necessity? Do we like the feeling of being "the person?" Is it a control issue?

All of the above, and more, are most likely true to a certain extent. But what is more important is what do we do about it. Regardless of the reasons that got us there, there is no reason we have to stay there. We are not victims. We make choices and have control over our decisions. So, if you sense this is where you are, or there are people around you telling you its where you are, be self-aware enough to recognize the situation and commit to making a change. Shift roles and responsibilities. Focus on your best fit and strengths. Talk to people about it. Tap into a mentor or an executive coach. Do what you need to do to break the pattern. You and your organization both deserve it.

Section Two: The Leader and Their Team

Chapter Six
Your Team Leader Role

Now that you are engaged and committed to a Learner's Mindset, becoming a Well-Defined Leader, growing in your Self Awareness, practicing the 5 Traits of Trusted Leadership, and having a clearer Role Focus, it's time to leverage that growth to transform the rest of your organization.

To review, leadership is the use of our social influence – our words and actions – to bring out the best in each person in order to bring out the best in our organizations. When it comes to bringing out the best in each person, there is no better place to start than your immediate team. That could be an executive team, a senior leadership team, a functional team—whatever team you lead is where we go next.

As a leader, you have a minimum of two roles to play on a team—the Team Leader and a Team Member. This chapter will address the role of Team Leader, with the following chapter focusing on the role of Team Member.

Emotional Safety

A key component of the Team Leader role is to provide for the group's emotional safety. What do I mean by emotional safety? I mean a place where people know it's okay to be open, honest, and vulnerable. Where folks can let their guard down and just be themselves. Where showing emotion isn't just accommodated but encouraged. Your team members have to know that participating in this manner not only won't bring negative consequences but is desired. Did you know that recent studies show that over 50% of employees are not willing to communicate their true feelings/emotions with leadership, and that almost 33% are unwilling to do so with their immediate co-workers? How in the world is a team going to be effective when half the room is holding back?

The role of the team leader starts with establishing and communicating the "rules of engagement" for the team and the importance of living them. More importantly, the leader must demonstrate consistent adherence to these rules of engagement. If you don't, no one else will. Like all things leadership related, it starts with the leader.

I recognize that, traditionally speaking, leadership and emotions don't necessarily go hand-in-hand. But as leaders, we need to be okay with this. Quick test: Is anger okay? Your initial response might be to say, "No, anger doesn't do any good in the workplace." But what is anger? It's a simple human emotion. The emotion isn't bad, but how we use it could be. It depends on if and how we give voice to it. If we try to hold it back, we fail to be fully engaged in the present. We disconnect from what's going on. If we turn our anger emotion into an attack on someone or something, giving it that voice is not productive either. But what if we give voice to it simply for what it is—an emotion? If we are operating in a safe environment that encourages honesty and transparency, then just say what you are feeling. It's okay to say something along the lines of, "The way this conversation is going is starting to make me angry, and I just needed to share that." Focus your voice not on who said the thing that prompted your anger emotion but what was said and why it triggered you. Maybe something said was received by you as unfair, or maybe it was incongruent with a stated core value. Putting it on the table will bring about openness and honesty reinforcing the desired rules of engagement.

The first time I shared a true emotion as a leader, I was quite surprised by the response I received. I was the COO of a firm and was meeting with the sales team to identify better ways to compensate for and incentivize sales. We went around the room putting ideas on the table for consideration, and when it was time for me to offer some ideas, I was met by a completely unexpected reaction. While I was offering my thoughts on how to provide additional incentives that the team never had before, the responses from the team focused on how they could "game the system" to earn the incentive without actually delivering the effort. After two or three tries at this, all my ideas met with similar responses, and I could feel the anger rising up inside of me. But instead of bottling this emotion up, I decided to give voice to it. What came out of my mouth surprised both me and the team. In a very measured but terse way, I said, "I have to tell you that right now I am completely pissed off at this team." That is a term that rarely crosses my lips, and this team had never heard that type of response out of me before. But here I was suggesting ways to grow the company that would generate greater income for them, and they were telling me how they could take advantage of the situation! I was angry! I suggested we break for 10 minutes, giving everyone a chance to process the previous conversation and come back to the table to discuss. In my 10 minutes, I was actually telling myself that I should not have shared my emotions that way, and I wasn't sure what the team response would be when we reconvened.

To my great surprise, when I got back to the room, everyone was already there. In fact, I'm not sure they ever left. The manager of the team spoke first. He thanked me for showing the emotion I did because for him it showed my passion for the business and getting it into a healthier place. The next person who spoke up shared that he realized the emotion I shared reminded him of the trust I had in the team and that their responses betrayed that trust. A few more comments followed and then we proceeded to have a very meaningful conversation about the different options, gaining the group's commitment to the best one, and moving forward in a way that benefited the organization and the sales team.

Another important element to providing for emotional safety for your team is to make sure each member's role and responsibilities are both understood and appreciated for the contributions they make to the organization's overall success. If a team member feels their role and contributions aren't understood by the rest of the team, they will not feel safe being open and honest in a team setting. By the same measure, if a team member feels that their contributions aren't at par with others on the team, they too will not feel safe to speak freely. As the team leader, your role includes making sure everyone understands the importance of each member's contributions to the team's performance. And you cannot allow any dialogue to the contrary. If they are in the room, they are there because they all play a critical role in the process. Sometimes this just needs to be said. Related to this is the team's understanding of what I call "the collective." As the team leader, it is critical that the team has an issue or opportunity to address that requires contributions from each member, i.e., the collective. It's an issue or challenge that cuts across all roles or functions in the room and is best served by pursuing it as a whole. There will always be items that don't require the full team involvement, but if you don't have one or two that impacts everyone, and would benefit from the collective process, then you may not be thinking big enough as the leader. This will not only bring all parties to the table, but it will help reinforce the rules of engagement that are in place to promote emotional safety.

Skills Required

As the Team Leader, you require a good number of skills to be effective. There are entire books written on this topic, so I just want to touch on three that I believe are most important.

First is the ability to Direct the Focus for the team. This starts with staying on purpose and in sync with strategic priorities. Any challenge a team is dealing with must be viewed through these lenses. How is what we are addressing helping us fulfill our organization's purpose and deliver against strategic priorities? This is where the team's energy needs to be directed. With one exception. If the pursuit of an issue gets sidelined due to a lot of energy suddenly coming to the surface for a seemingly unrelated topic, you may want to follow that energy to a point. If not, moving back on topic may be a fruitless exercise if folks are still on the new topic. You may find the energy is actually around an underlying issue that could stand in the way of achieving your initial goal. In this case, the skill is to follow the energy in the room until it makes sense to redirect back to the original topic while recognizing and appreciating the energy that bubbled up on the unplanned topic.

For the leader to be effective at Directing the Focus, they first must be successful at directing their own focus. Coming into the meeting with the team, clear your mind of other issues and potential distractions. If you are distracted, the team will be distracted. If you can't stay on point, neither will the team. So, get yourself aligned first.

The second skill I want to touch on is the ability to Regulate Stress and Anxiety. Certain issues and challenges are sure to affect the anxiety level of the team members. Your role is to ensure there is not too much, or too little, stress in the system at any given time. This means there are times you may need to call a timeout and allow for the stress level to come down, and there may be times when you need to inject a little anxiety into the team to get the appropriate level of focus and energy. Think of this as like an old-fashioned thermostat in your home or office. The thermostat allows you to "set" the temperature, or level of anxiety you believe is appropriate for the team. But you need to keep your eye on the temperature reading to make sure it's tracking with what you set. If the temperature reading is a little low, turn up the setting. If it's running a little hot, bring the setting down a bit. Just like in the Emotional Safety discussion, where you are responsible for establishing a safe "container" for the team, you also are responsible for ensuring the container temperature is where it should be.

The third and last skill we'll discuss is the ability to Frame the Issue. Framing is simply a means of presenting a challenge or issue for the team. It requires context setting, with the goal of describing context in a way that is clear to the team and motivates them. When framing an issue or challenge, the audience – in this case your team – is key. The problem must be posed in a way that generates the desired response from the team. Focus on the "why" of the challenge—describing why it exists, why it must be solved, and why it must be solved now.

Let me provide a brief example. Years back, my consulting team voiced their concern that I made a decision to take on work for a client in an area outside of our traditional service offerings for the sake of revenue only. On the surface it could appear that way, as the scope of this work involved a review of compensation and benefits while our core work was in the area of organizational culture. To do the work, we would need to subcontract the technical aspects to a firm that specializes in the areas of compensation and benefits, which made it look like a complete misfit for us. The frame I had to use was that compensation and benefit policies directly impacted organizational culture, and since we were hired to improve culture, we should be directly involved in any recommendations and decisions to change policies around compensation. That's what I mean by framing.

If you have practiced framing issues before, then you know a related skill that is definitely a necessity—the ability to reframe. If the first frame isn't working, recognize that and reframe the issue the best you can. If the first frame didn't resonate with the team, it's time to look at the problem from a different vantage point or perspective. The more you practice framing, the better you will get at it, to the point of doing so without even thinking about it.

Chapter Seven
Your Team Member Role

Participating as a member of a team while at the same time being an organizational leader is much more complicated than it sounds. If you've tried it, you have to agree. As leaders, we know the value of collective problem solving and group creativity. But how do we keep from squelching that energy when we are part of a team that includes subordinates? All we want is for them to simply treat us like any other member of the team, right? Except we're not, especially from their perspective. Here are a few ideas to help you, the leader, in this role.

Remember Who You Are, Because *They* Do

First off is a dose of reality. Despite your best intentions and efforts to be "just another member of a team", the reality is that no one else will ultimately see you that way. Surprised? I know, we've heard all the familiar expressions that attempt to dismiss this reality: "Let's leave our titles at the door", "We are going to suspend status", "Around this table, we are all equal", etc. But guess what? If you have organizational authority and utilize it the other 364 days of the year, you will be viewed with authority this day as well. We are only fooling ourselves if we believe otherwise. I learned this lesson time and time again, as I kept trying to convince myself that suspending status was possible.

At first, I was naïve enough to think that if I just altered my approach, others would interact with me differently. So, I would try my best to listen more and speak less, intentionally trying to add my thoughts last. And, of course, in a way that I was convinced was coming across as a suggestion and not a directive. Guess how that went! The team would instantly act as if my thought trumped all others, and after that new ideas were tough to find. But I told them, in all sincerity, that it was just my idea for the team's consideration. Why don't they respond that way? Because my role to that point, and every day outside of that room, was one of authority. And they remind you of this by saying things like "Well, you are the managing partner, so we assumed that's how you wanted the team to proceed."

Based on that failed attempt I figured a better, more convincing, approach was required. I thought if I reminded them in a practical way that I was participating as a team member, and not the leader, we could get past the authority issue. Still naïve, I decided I would make everyone aware when going into a discussion or meeting that for this discussion I was "taking off my partner hat" and participating as a member of the team. All comments and ideas were equal, and mine carried no more weight than the others because, of course, I had taken off my partner hat. I did it right there in front of them. This had to be more effective, right? Of course not! It was still me in the chair—the same guy who makes decisions around hiring, firing, pricing, strategy, priorities, etc., etc., etc. I still remember having the conversation with one of my partners; expressing my frustration over how the team couldn't function with me as just another member. And he laughed at me! Deservedly! I even told him about taking off my partner hat. He laughed harder. Finally, he looked at me and asked the obvious, "Why would you think they could see you as anything other than their boss, since that is what you are?" But I so wanted them to. I was convinced I could make them see me that way. It would all work out ideally. Good gracious, I was naïve!

So, step one: rather than believing you can convince everyone to treat you like every other member of the team, accept the reality that this will not be the case. The sooner you realize this, the better. Then you can move on to how best to operate in a team member role, knowing that you bring your authority with you and everyone else knows it.

Watch Your Words

Now that we've established that suspending status and leaving your title at the door is impossible, let's focus on our words and actions, given they come from a person with authority. I believe our words in these scenarios are so, so incredibly important—everything from what we say, how we say it, and even what we *don't* say. In an instant, with the wrong word or tone, you can throw away weeks of progress in functioning more like a team member. The moment you state something as a directive instead of input for consideration, it's all over. You truly have to be error-free in this regard. Being self-aware of your feelings and emotions and recognizing if you are located in the red zone or blue zone become more important than ever. If frustration or impatience manifests itself in your explicit or implicit use of authority, it will bring everything positive to this point to a screeching halt.

When I was the COO of a consulting firm, our president decided we would take a team approach to hiring the next class of consultants. We had a handful of candidates come to our office and the president, I, and three other senior leaders interviewed them, one-to-one in round-robin fashion. We each had roughly an hour with each candidate, after which our team would meet for two hours to compare notes and calibrate the candidates. The plan was for the five of us to discuss each candidate, one at a time, and conclude on whether we wanted to make them an offer of not. It was a fine plan. So, after our six hours of interviews, we were all excited to get into a room and start sharing what we learned. Right before we teed up the conversation on the first candidate, the president said the following: "I know our goal is to hire 3 or 4 of these folks and we're going to talk about each one of them, but I want you to know regardless of what you say I really like Candidate X and we are going to hire him." Guess what happened to the energy in the room? Yep, right out the window. He injected his authority into the process and immediately everyone else felt that their thoughts from the day were going to be completely dismissed. But he said it with a smile on his face. Even laughed after he said it. Doesn't that matter? He obviously didn't really mean it, did he? Guess what, it doesn't matter. He is in a position of authority and when he said it, regardless of how he said it, the authority came across. It's kind of like a strong odor. You can try to camouflage it with sprays and scents, but it still comes through regardless, even if it smells a little better.

So again, we as leaders must be error-free in this regard. One simple misstep is all it takes to remind people of who is in charge and whose opinions matter more than others. Not only is all momentum lost, but as we talked about on the subject of trust, it is so hard to earn this back once lost. Even if you are better the next time, the team will tend to remember your mistake and the impact it had on them. So be careful with your words!

Get on the Same Side of the Table
One practice that will help the leader participate more like a team member is the simple idea of physical positioning. If you bring a team together, including yourself, to do collective work on an issue or challenge, the first thing you want to do is get on the same side of the table as the rest of the team. Literally.

Nothing squelches the collective team spirit like the leader standing in the front of the room with a marker in their hand. You cannot participate as a facilitator and contributor at the same time. So, take your pick. For the sake of the collective effort, I recommend you give up the facilitator role and join the rest of the team at the table.

You have a few options here. Ideally, if the situation warrants it, having an independent facilitator is the best way to go. It doesn't need to be a hired consultant, but having an expert facilitator is well worth the investment. This is especially true if you are dealing with weighty issues like vision, core values, strategic imperatives, organizational design, etc.

The second option is to bring in a co-worker with facilitation experience, who works in another group or function. Take advantage of skills that exist in your organization without incurring incremental hard costs. The benefit is they have the organizational context without necessarily having opinions on the matter at hand. To ensure there are no misunderstandings or functional tension, make sure your team understands why this person is facilitating. This plan also serves as a good way to give exposure to people or functions that otherwise would not occur, which is healthy for all organizations.

The third option, as a last resort, is to simply share or rotate the facilitator role across the team members in the room. Some may be more comfortable or experienced than others, which is OK. You can allow people to pass on the opportunity, but make sure it is understood that all are invited to participate in that manner. I would recommend that you, the leader, pass on the role as long as you have others that can carry the load. This option allows for a true sharing of responsibility while providing an opportunity for individuals to develop their leadership and facilitation capacity.

That wraps up this chapter on your role with teams. The main takeaway is that how you function can't be the perception in your own head and it can't be based on a statement you make—it has to be from your consistent actions.

Chapter Eight
Strengths-Based Teams

This is a topic I am extremely passionate about, and the leader plays such a vital role in having strengths-based teams in their organizations. There is no better way to bring out the best in people and teams than to focus on strengths. Organizations have spent decades pursuing the opposite approach, with poor results to show for it in terms of our people's development.

Historically, most organizations have development plans and efforts focused on a person's "opportunities", better described as the areas in which someone is not performing to standard. We identify these on an annual basis, agree to a plan for improvement, and come back 12 months later acting surprised that these areas are still "opportunities." First of all, if these areas are not natural strengths for us, chances are the best we will ever get at them is "at standard", or average. Is this really where we want to be spending a lot of time and energy?

I worked with a Fortune 50 company for 16 years, and the exercise never changed. Every year, three areas were identified as opportunities, and a creative plan was devised to help me develop in these areas. I would love to tell you that those areas are now towering strengths for me, but that would be a lie. I'm sure I became average at them, but I'm not sure becoming average enabled me to make substantially greater contributions to the organization. But we did spend a fair amount of time, energy, and money—making me average in those areas, for which I'm convinced the shareholders were extremely grateful!

How often have you participated in a year-end appraisal or development discussion that focused on what your strengths were and how to further develop and deploy them? Ever? Me neither, and it's a shame. We are all born with, and develop in our early years, specific talents that become our strengths. It's part of what makes us unique, and in order to apply those to our unique purpose in life, we have to focus on them and maximize them.

For a leader to Form, Build, and Sustain teams based on strengths, they must become schooled on the topic AND fully understand, appreciate, and leverage their own strengths first. We touched on this topic in the first section of this book, and we will return to it here to ensure that you, as the leader, have the proper bandwidth in this area to lead the effort.

I am a 100% disciple of Gallup's StrengthsFinder assessment tool and process, so I'll recommend two things right off the bat. First, pick up the book *StrengthsFinder 2.0*, written by Tom Rath. This will provide you with the context needed for leveraging strengths for yourself and your teams. Second, take the online StrengthsFinder assessment found on the Gallup website. It costs $20 and will take less than 30 minutes, and you will be provided with a summary of your "Top 5 Talents." If you really want to dig in, pay a little more and you can receive the rank order of all 34 StrengthsFinder talents.

Since I also utilize other assessment tools in my work, both commercial and proprietary, I don't want to discount those. They all serve a specific purpose, and in the case of StrengthsFinder, that purpose is to help people realize that leadership is all about leveraging the strengths you have. Everyone can lead effectively if they do so with an understanding of their natural talents and take full advantage of them. Other tools like DISC, MBI, Enneagrams, etc. can be effective in understanding behaviors and personality traits, but StrengthsFinder is the only tool that focuses on what you are good at — your natural talents.

When you, the leader, receive your Top 5 Talents, you will also receive tools to assist you in understanding and appreciating them. This learning about ourselves is so very important. For some that I have worked with over the years, it can be a watershed moment when connections are made for the first time about their experiences in both work and home life. Trust me, there will be "aha" moments. This path of self-discovery leads to growth, and growth to transformation, so please don't skip or rush it. Part of the process I recommend is to discuss these talents with your coworkers, friends, and families. Explain to them what each one means, and how each talent manifests itself, using the report received. Ask them for their honest feedback. Do you believe these are my top talents? Why do you say so? How do you experience them in me? This is especially true if you are personally struggling with any of your Top 5. Rather than denying it or dismissing it, ask others if they see it in you. You most likely will be surprised by what their take is, versus your own. There is so much more detail we could get into here, but if you read the book and take the time to process your results, you will be ready to work with your teams. To help you do this, I will focus on three phases: Forming, Building, and Sustaining Strengths-Based Teams. As a leader, this will be one of the most important things you will ever do.

Forming Strengths-Based Teams
When putting teams together, whether they are intact/functional teams or project-based teams, you will want to make strengths part of the profile considered. I'm not saying that we should make hiring decisions and team assignments based on strengths alone, but it should be included in the assessment of "fit", along with culture/values alignment, competency, etc.

As I mentioned, the StrengthsFinder assessment looks at a set of 34 natural talents or strengths. Given the millions of potential combinations, it's extremely unlikely that someone you know has the same talents in their top five, not to mention in the same order of 1 through 5. This supports my belief that we are all uniquely made, and for a unique purpose. But in putting a team together, you do want as much diversity across the talents as possible. This ensures the broadest set of perspectives while protecting against potential blind spots. Think of it the same way a baseball manager approaches their batting lineup. While left-handed power hitters are great to have in your lineup, you don't want nine of them. Instead, you want a mix of right-handed and left-handed batters—some who hit for average and some who hit for power. It's the right mix that is the most effective.

When I was brought into a ten-year-old partnership, one of the key things they looked at were my strengths. The existing partners were like-minded friends, which is one reason they got into business together in the first place. But over time they realized the need for talents that were not represented by the existing partners. So not only did my experience, abilities, and cultural alignment fit the role they had in mind, but they highly valued the fact that I brought several talents in my top 5 that they didn't possess. Which leads me to a second point about the importance of strengths consideration in forming teams.

In the case of project or short-term teams, the nature of the work or the outcome desired may very well put a premium on certain strengths as opposed to others. I'm not going to get into all 34 talents here (you can find that in the *StrengthsFinder 2.0* book by Rath), but I do want to stress that while all strengths are "equal", the work sometimes will require you to "check the box" on certain ones. A simple example would be a project that required a great deal of data and analysis. There is a strength that goes by the name "Analytical"; in this example, you would not want to form a project team that didn't have a strong presence of this talent. Again, this is just an example. It's more important that the concept of strengths diversity and matching is making sense to you. From there, the application is pretty straightforward.

Building Strengths-Based Teams

The building of strengths-based teams has to do with you, the leader, making sure the team you formed understands and appreciates the importance of leveraging their strengths. This starts with the entire group getting up to speed on the strength-based methodology and becoming aware of their own strengths.

I currently deliver, and my prior organization did as well, a workshop titled "Prevailing Talents." It is intended for any team that wants to become a stronger, more impactful team. Depending on the size of the team, it could be a one or two-day workshop. You, the leader, would be part of that team workshop, with the expectation that you leverage the learning throughout the year with your team.

The benefits of this type of workshop are many. First, it's another vehicle for getting your team together and learning together. This builds trust. Second, the strengths-based methodology will provide the team with a new and common language. Third, by the end of the workshop, each team member will come to realize that every person has unique gifts and talents, and they are all valuable to the overall success of the team. We need to not only understand the gifts of others but celebrate them!

The workshop starts with a review of each team member's top 5 talents—allowing the individual to discuss their thoughts and allowing others to respond by providing examples of how they see those talents displayed (or not). If you want to make it a little more fun, we leave the person's name off the page that lists the talents and ask folks to guess who they think it could be. This works well for teams that have been together for a little while.

Once everyone has had the opportunity to have a conversation about their strengths, I like to have them work through a number of exercises to make sure they understand and appreciate their own strengths as well as those of others. I like to put folks in groups that have like talents to discuss how they see similarities and differences. Also, I'll ask a subgroup to explain to those without their talents what types of communication and information would be most useful to them so that others will understand that the way they prefer things isn't always the same as others prefer them. Again, there is a lot you can do here to help the concept and specifics stick, all of which can mix in a little fun.

Once the team grasps the fundamentals of the individual talents and is learning how to appreciate each other's top 5, we move onto aggregate team talents. By this I mean what a team top 5 looks like. This is simply based on the number of times a strength exists across the group. For example, the strength that is most present in the team members' individual top 5 becomes the team's number one talent, the next most present is number two, and so on to create the team top 5. This provides the team with an understanding of their collective strengths and indicates what type of work or projects they could be best suited for. It could also point out the need for greater diversity as well.

When I say diversity from a team perspective, in addition to what was mentioned in the previous section on forming teams there is one other aspect I would like to bring up. And again, we'll stay at the conceptual level in order to not go deep into strengths methodology here. The simple concept is this: across the 34 talents, some naturally group together. Some are more self-focused, while some have a greater focus on those around us. Some are more about thinking and processing, while others lean more towards action and motivation. I cover this in much greater detail in workshops, but the key is understanding that the more a team has strengths that group into one or two types, the less they will benefit from the perspectives of the types of strengths not present. For example, if a team consists of a high number of members with talents that tend to lean towards internal thinking and processing, but don't have talents that are more action-oriented, this could prove to be problematic. It's possible the group could spend an inordinate amount of time assessing while struggling to get to decisions and activity. The leader, and the team, need to be aware of this as a potential blind spot.

There is so much more I could get into on the topic of building strengths-based teams, but for now we'll leave it right here. My goal is not to make you an expert on strengths, but for you to hopefully see strengths as another element of fit; another aspect of diversity that's worth investing in as you build your teams.

Sustaining Strengths-Based Teams

Now that you have formed your strengths-based team and invested time in building and developing it, the hard work is done, right? I'm afraid not. The most important and valuable effort will involve sustaining and leveraging the uniqueness of the team.

First up is ensuring you always have folks in the right roles—the proverbial "right seat on the bus", especially as team objectives and deliverables change. Over time you will want to continuously look at the work you have, overlay it with the people you have, and make sure you are leveraging strengths to optimize roles. Too many times we leave people in roles for no other reason than it's the role they have always been in. Work changes and, along with it, capabilities and strengths; it's not just OK to consider shifts in roles but encouraged. This communicates that you are committed to structuring resources in ways that put the team and individuals first. One positive byproduct of this, along with better alignment with strengths and fit, is that these moves provide folks with new challenges and opportunities. It helps keep people and work from getting "stale." Another positive byproduct is that by doing some shifting of roles, you "cross-pollenate" knowledge across the team, providing yourself with natural fallback plans if needed. If someone were to suddenly leave your organization, not all of the knowledge associated with their area of responsibility will walk out the door with them. And last but not least, shifts that make sense for the business and the individual will naturally require team members to tap into each other more, fostering greater collaboration. So, bottom line—don't hesitate to shift roles to be in better alignment with strengths. Work can be a long and bumpy bus ride if you are in the wrong seat!

Next, make sure you integrate a conversation about strengths into every performance and development discussion. On an annual basis, be sure to include how the individual is or isn't leveraging their strengths in their day-to-day work. Do they feel they are optimizing them? What could change that? What experiences could further develop their strengths? If you normally do monthly or quarterly check-ins on performance and development plans, make it a part of those discussions as well (if you're not doing regular performance and development check-ins throughout the year, it's time to start!). This also reinforces the new language being developed around strengths for team members.

The last topic involves new members of the team. When you experience turnover, make sure the new team member is immersed in the strengths-based approach from day one. As mentioned previously, make it part of the hiring assessment and decision. Introduce how team strengths are leveraged as part of their onboarding. Provide them with all of the team strengths information that others have received to that point. The last thing you want is for the group to be speaking a language that the newest hire doesn't understand. It's like being in a foreign country and unable to speak the native language. Think of when you have traveled abroad and just how difficult and frustrating that can be. Don't let this happen on your team.

In this chapter, I've tried to provide an overview of a strengths-based approach to teams. Not to make you an expert—that takes time. But hopefully to make the point that, as a leader looking for an engaged, high-functioning team, the concept of leveraging strengths is vital to your team's performance ... as well as your own.

Chapter Nine
High-Functioning Teams

There is much great research and writing on the subject of team performance. I am a huge believer in teams and the impact high-functioning teams can have, and I have spent three decades aspiring to build healthy teams as the basis for organizational impact. Steve Jobs once said, "Great things in business are never done by one person. They are done by a team of people." I couldn't agree more!

First off, let's distinguish high-functioning teams from other collections of co-workers. At the most rudimentary level is what I'll call a "work group." A work group is organized under a common supervisor on an organization chart, typically all within a single functional area. But it is a work group – not a team – because the individuals have independent objectives and goals, aren't interdependent, and don't approach challenges as a collective. In a lot of cases, some don't even fully understand what others in the group do. It makes no sense, in this case, to try to form a high-functioning team. It's not necessary nor would it be productive.

The other alternative I've encountered in workplaces is what I'll call an "imitation team." This is a group of individuals who have all the reasons to be operating as a high-functioning team, but they are not. Yet, they *think* they are! This is the most dangerous scenario by far. The leader and members genuinely believe they are operating as a team, but none of the attributes associated with teams are present. Members of these groups inevitably act as though everyone is in alignment and working together towards a common goal when the reality is the complete opposite. This can cause frustration, dysfunction, inefficiency, and, in the worst case, complete failure for the business or a function of the business. How do you know if you have an imitation team? For starters, the following qualities of a high-functioning team are not present.

Five Qualities of a High-Functioning Team

I have found, and others such as Pat MacMillan, Patrick Lencioni, and Richard Hackman have arrived at similar conclusions, that there are a handful of fundamental qualities or traits that are necessary to have a high-functioning team. These are simply what I have found in my experience to be necessary for teams to perform at their best. They are:

1) Foundation of Trust
2) Healthy Conflict
3) Committed Alignment
4) Mutual Accountability
5) Measurement and Celebration of Successes

Foundation of Trust

In the first section of this book, we talked about the "5 Traits of Trusted Leadership", and the importance of trust in leadership. The traits included Care, Character, Communication, Capacity, and Consistency. These same traits must be present across a team for performance to be at its highest level. Rather than revisit what's been shared, let's focus on how teams can develop these traits. We know what trust looks and feels like, right? So, let's talk about ways to build it. If you need a refresher, please refer back to Chapter Four.

As mentioned, trust takes years to build, seconds to break, and forever to repair. So, when it comes to teams you have to be committed to the time and effort this will take. One thing that can help accelerate the timeframe is if the leader themselves has already modeled the traits for the team on a consistent basis. That context and example can go a long way when the leader sets out to develop a high-functioning team. But, bottom line, this will take significant time and energy, and it cannot be rushed. I want you to keep two words in mind: space and pace. As the leader, you will need to provide space for this development to occur and to assess the appropriate pace for the team, given variables like size of team and existing relationships. What might seem slow to you for one team may actually be fast for another. Each will have their own pace.

As far as space is concerned, you will want to get your team away from their work/workplace in order to allow them to focus 100% on the effort, and do so on a committed, regular schedule. At first, you may want to take one day per month for a few months to build momentum. As you progress you can back off to something along the lines four times per year. Dedicate at least a full day without regular work seeping into the day. To achieve a full day with an early start, I strongly recommend a dinner or social event the evening before. This serves as an ice breaker for folks and allows for relationships to begin/evolve. I know there are a hundred reasons why you can't afford a full day and include something the evening before, but you just have to do this. I promise you will not regret it. If you are serious about team performance, you have to be serious about providing the proper space for it to be developed.

Regarding pace, you as the leader must take care not to rush or proceed too slowly with the group. You can only determine this by monitoring the behaviors of the team members. Appropriate pace will vary by individual, so your goal is to find the happy medium. If folks seem to be going through the motions or trying to win a race, then slow them down. If they are chasing rabbits down unrelated trails and getting lost in minutiae, you can pick it up. The key is to be sensitive to this. It doesn't really matter where you think the group should be. The pace will be the pace, and your role is to regulate it.

That said, let's move onto some examples of building trust. The fundamental principle here is that people can't trust people they don't know. And I don't mean know them professionally — they have to know them as a person. This involves being vulnerable with people, maybe in ways team members have not done before. So, start out with some simple exercises and build on them over time. Here are some that I use:

- <u>Favorites</u> – ask each person to share their favorite something. If its summertime, ask each person to describe their favorite summer vacation spot. If it's a holiday season, ask people to share their favorite holiday movie. Ask everyone to share what they would do if they had a whole day for themselves. There is no magic question here. The goal is to get everyone talking and listening. The easier the question the better, at first. These can be done in a large group, as each person's response only takes a minute or two.

- <u>Sentence Stems</u> – this one works best in groups of up to eight people, so feel free to assign groups of eight. The beauty is you can do this multiple times throughout the day, mixing the groups up. The way this works is every group is given the same sentence stem, or starting phrase, and each person shares their sentence completion within their group. For example, an easy starting sentence stem is, "Being here today makes me feel..." Then each person takes turns stating the stem and completing it with their own thoughts. So, one might say, "Being here today makes me feel a little nervous." Another might say, "Being here today makes me feel excited that we are working on becoming a stronger team." There is no discussion of each person's response, but instead just work your way around the group, giving everyone a chance to complete the stem. As the group gets to know each other a little better, you can progress to sentence stems like "I'm at my best when...." or "My superpower is...." or "One thing you should know about me is..." You get the idea. There really is no limit to stems you can come up with, but just make sure the information required to complete the stem

is aligned with the current level of trust in the group.
- <u>Interviews</u> – this example allows two individuals to go deep in getting to know each other while providing the broader group with the benefit of their interaction. I like to provide an interview form with 4 to 6 questions and have two team members take turns interviewing each other and capturing their responses. Again, the questions can be as light or heavy as you believe the existing trust will allow. Simple ones include where folks were born, number of siblings, etc. More interesting ones could be questions about important experiences in their lives, what matters most to them, etc.
- <u>Pictionary Introductions</u> – this one is a little different but is a twist on people saying something about themselves. Instead of saying it, have each person draw it. Give each person a flipchart-sized paper and have them draw the answer to a question. It gets people on their feet and sharing in a different medium, which can be fun to see. For example, ask people to answer the question, "What three things matter most to you?" and have them draw the answer. You will see everything from stick figure families, to churches with steeples, to drawings of pets. You'll learn about each other's interests, not to mention getting to have fun with people's artistic abilities!

Again, these serve to have people get to know each other a little better because we can't trust those we don't know. Once we are comfortable sharing this level of information about ourselves with the team, we are on our way to being vulnerable with each other. **Vulnerability is the soil in which trust can grow.** When we are vulnerable, we start naturally doing things that benefit the team, like asking for help, sharing concerns, and admitting shortcomings or mistakes.

Beyond establishing trust through caring and vulnerability, the two other dimensions of trust I want to discuss are Credibility and Dependability. Both of these attributes are connected to the Character Trait we covered in section 1.

Credibility simply means that people can believe in what you say. Teams don't need a member that knows everything but instead needs members who *do* know what they should, given their respective roles. If a team member has skill and experience in a particular area, then others will want to hear what they have to say and believe what they share. A person with credibility is a resource that can be relied on; someone whom others will be comfortable with when making a decision on behalf of the team. Charisma can aid credibility at times but can never replace it. By the same token, your charisma travels with you from role to role and team to team, but credibility doesn't always travel well. For example, if you have been a successful sales and marketing executive who gets promoted to a Chief Operating Officer role, you will need to generate credibility in the operational aspects of the business before you have credibility and are trusted in this area.

Dependability differs from credibility in that credibility is about belief in what you express while dependability is based on what you do—your actions. In the context of teams, people that are dependable are reliable. They do what they say they are going to do, without exception. Dependable people don't make promises they cannot keep. If you are dependable, chances are you have a high degree of responsibility. Your word is your oath. Everybody wants to work with people like this, and everyone quickly learns they can trust people like this.

To wrap up this first quality of high-functioning teams, a foundation of trust, if team members can focus on vulnerability, credibility, and dependability while avoiding the appearance of self-interest, the team is off to a great start. You will want consistency in these areas, so stay focused on them with your team.

Healthy Conflict
Read this statement. **Conflict in teams is good.** Do you agree or disagree with it? How about this one. **Lack of conflict in teams is an indicator of high team cohesion.** Agree or disagree? Not sure? As a leader, you want teams to have a healthy dose of conflict. It's a good thing. Where your role comes into play is ensuring it's "healthy."

Why do you want conflict? Because, without it, your team will never move on to the next quality of high-functioning teams—Committed Alignment. Oh, and what is required in order to have a team engage in healthy conflict? You guessed it, a Foundation of Trust. Yes, these qualities build on each other. Team members will only engage in open, honest conflict with those they trust—those they can be vulnerable with and visa-versa. Let's start with what *unhealthy* conflict looks like since most of us are more familiar with this than with the healthy variety.

Below are the typical behaviors associated with unhealthy conflict. Again, I borrow from and acknowledge the work done by my friends Messrs. Jurkowski and Osterhaus:

- Disengagement – I retreat to avoid
- Easily Annoyed – I react immediately and negatively
- Become Resentful – I believe I'm being treated unfairly
- Personal Attacks – I defend self by attacking others
- Procrastination – I put off seemingly negative things
- Story Telling – I make assumptions and tell myself stories
- Escalation – I get more intense

Now there are a lot of reasons, psychologically and physically, why we behave in these ways. But for the sake of this discussion, we will stay focused on the outward behaviors and the differences in them between unhealthy and healthy conflict. Here are the alternative behaviors normally observed with healthy conflict:

- Thoughtfulness – I stay engaged
- Reflective – I pause and respond vs. immediately reacting
- Become Curious – I listen for underlying issues
- Personal Grace – I don't assume negative intentions
- Clarification – I ask questions to better understand
- Story Checking – I check my assumptions and stories
- Reframing – I view the situation in a more positive manner

Unhealthy conflict will always stem from behaviors that are "me" focused, while healthy conflict behaviors will come from an "us" perspective. These are typically easy to identify for a leader and then pivot from. Some things to consider when trying to shift to healthy conflict:

- Have the group work with more information than less
- Encourage debate solely based on facts
- Develop multiple alternatives vs. yes/no to enrich the discussion
- Refer back to the business goals and objectives
- Inject a little humor into the process
- Don't overplay your power; now is time to facilitate
- Resolve issues without forcing unanimity

Over time, a high-functioning team will naturally lean toward healthy conflict, but in the beginning, it will be incumbent on the leader to assess what is unhealthy vs.

healthy; to be able to model and require the behaviors necessary to shift. When it comes to teams, I believe healthy conflict is of the utmost importance.

Committed Alignment

If your team is practicing healthy conflict, you have a leg up on gaining the next quality of high-functioning teams, Committed Alignment. To describe what this looks like, I'll start with the second word, alignment. I like to tell leaders that one of their primary roles is to be the team chiropractor, always looking to identify possible misalignment and getting the team back into alignment. This applies to one-time challenges like a specific initiative the team is tasked with, or it could be a long-term effort dealing with team alignment around core principles or values.

For a team to be aligned, every member needs to be heard. That is why healthy conflict is so critical. Once all perspectives are shared, and the alternatives debated in a healthy manner, it is the leader who then must move the team toward alignment. The goal is not to achieve unanimity but to gain alignment around the best approach forward. In the pursuit of alignment, the leader must make the connection between this decision at hand and the overarching purpose and goals of the team and organization. Alignment is based on "why" this solution is the best path forward and "how" it fits with purpose, values, and goals. The dots have to be connected, and the leader gets to do this.

Once you've established alignment, you have succeeded in getting the team members' "minds" in the same place. Now it's time to get their "hearts" there as well. To do so, we return to the first word in this quality, commitment. You most likely will not have total agreement on the decisions made, but you definitely will need total commitment. Once decisions are made, for the team to be successful there simply cannot be hesitation, second-guessing, or pocket vetoes. What was decided by the team must be committed to by all its members. A weak link will cause the chain to break.

One potential reason for team members not being fully committed could be a lack of clarity or some ambiguity about the team's direction. If this is the case, the leader must identify it and address it. It's as simple as asking the question, "Is there anything that needs to be clarified about the decision made and the direction we are heading as a team?" Work through any issues brought up, confirming that the additional information you provided clears up the specific ambiguity. Take your time with this, while letting the team know that once clarifications are provided the expectation is that the team will move forward in full committed alignment.

Another reason for commitment being withheld is resistance. There may be very good reasons for resistance, so you will want to use resistance as your friend. Leaning into resistance will allow you to understand the real reason behind it. You want to know this. The worst thing you can do as a leader is to ignore the resistance and try to move past it. It doesn't go away; it will always be there. Now is the time to shed light on it.

Think of reasons why you have resisted things in the past. We all have done it. One reason, and the most basic of reasons, is change. If the team has decided on a new approach that includes new responsibilities for members, change is happening. And with change comes loss for people, loss of how things used to be. This makes us anxious. The best thing a leader can do in this case is to listen to, and appreciate, what is being shared. Be careful not to dismiss it as unimportant, because it *is* to the person sharing it. In some cases, you may be able to mitigate some of the loss by suggesting an adjustment to the approach. In most cases, allowing the member to give voice to their concern, and acknowledging it, will be the path forward. A good tactic I've used at times is to ask the rest of the team if they have the same concern. If there is a lot of concern, then you may need to go back to the approach as a team. If there is no one else who shares the same concern, it helps the individual and the group move forward.

Other possible reasons for resistance could include fear of failure, risk aversion, lack of confidence in the team or specific individuals, and the possibility of additional work. All of these reasons are real to the person or persons expressing them, regardless of what you think. Aren't you better off knowing that team members feel this way now, rather than it manifesting itself in worse ways later? Hear them all out, appreciate that it is being shared, and don't be afraid to show a little empathy. You can be transparent and share your own feelings as well.

With ambiguity and resistance addressed and cared for, you are now in a position to ask, very specifically, for everyone's commitment. Acknowledge that things may be difficult and new information may arise that requires the team to revisit certain decisions, but upon leaving this conversation there must be committed alignment from all members in order for the team to be successful. If it is a matter of high importance, I suggest you have each person voice their commitment, because it is this commitment that will allow for our next quality of a high-functioning team, Mutual Accountability.

Mutual Accountability
The fourth quality of high-functioning teams is Mutual Accountability. It's a straightforward concept that can be extremely difficult to exercise for teams. But if you have a team with a solid foundation of trust, that engages in healthy conflict, and that has committed alignment, you are ready to develop an environment of mutual accountability. To bring about this type of environment we will focus on three things you must do as the leader: authorize it, enable it, and model it.

We'll start with authorizing mutual accountability. This simply means that you, as the leader, are describing the behavior and establishing it as a principle to be applied across the team. What behavior are you looking for? You want every member of the team to hold each other responsible for the commitments they made to the team and to each other. Members are going to provide feedback to each other, both positive and negative, in a consistent, respectful manner. You as the leader will not be the only person doing this. It's up to everyone and it's reciprocal. Make the connection between mutual accountability and achieving team goals and objectives. It is vital that the team understands that you expect mutual accountability and what it looks like when practiced. Gain commitment from the team to this all-important quality.

Next, you have to enable mutual accountability. Let's go back to what you authorized. You want every member of the team to hold each other responsible for the commitments they made to the team and each other. Pretty clear right? Conceptually, yes. But to put it into practice, the first thing needed is clear assignments and expectations for each member of the team. People can only hold each other accountable for those things we know are their specific responsibilities. So, step one of enabling mutual accountability is to make sure each member of the team understands their specific assignments and the assignments of others. If not, there can be no accountability. Worse yet, members may try to hold others accountable for things that are not their responsibility, which compounds the problem. Next up in enabling mutual accountability is to foster as much collaboration as possible. By fostering collaboration, members will become more aware of each other's assignments, the status or progress being made on them, and the interdependencies of one person's work with that of another member. This makes mutual accountability more accessible and impactful, and it gives the team greater ownership over the work and outcomes.

Last, and not least, is the leader's role in modeling what mutual accountability looks like for the team. As I've said many times already, leaders get to go first. In this case, there are two aspects of going first I want to focus on. First, model how to hold yourself accountable. How do you do that? Simple—do the things you said you would do, do them well, and do them on time. That's what you expect from everyone else, right? So set the example for the team. Establish a standard. We said that leadership is a "social thing"; that people watch us and listen to us all the time. Well, they'll be watching here for sure. Second, model how to hold others accountable. This will help others, who may initially find calling out their peers a bit uncomfortable, understand how to do so effectively. The approaches and techniques suggested in the next paragraph apply equally to both positive and negative accountability and feedback. Most of us think of accountability as calling out peers for underperformance but establishing a culture of positive feedback is critical as well.

First and foremost, always remember these conversations are about the work—not the person. If someone fails to meet a deadline, that doesn't make them a failure. Focus on the tasks and not the individual. With that as our starting point, include three things in each conversation: **context, specifics, and impact**. For context, let them know why you are approaching them. For example, "Mary, I want to talk about Project X that we are working on and provide feedback on Assignment Y that you are delivering." For specifics, be factual and timely. Refer to a specific responsibility that is not being met and do so as close to the due date as possible. For example, "John, Task Z, which you committed to having completed by yesterday, hasn't been delivered as of noon today." Don't assume anything. If you're not sure about any aspect of the work, ask first. Last, share what the impact on you and/or the team is. Keep it professional and focused on team goals and objectives. For instance, "Sue, not delivering on your commitment to having your task completed as of the close of business yesterday will require my team to work over the weekend in hopes of getting the project back on track." Always keep in mind that mutual accountability is reciprocal, so how you address it with your peers can have an effect on how they, in turn, bring things to your attention.

The final topic on Mutual Accountability I want to mention is how to stay out of the trap of being the only person holding others accountable. To make this point, I am going to utilize what is referred to as "relationship triangles." In particular, I will use "The Drama Triangle", based on the work of Stephen Karpman. In admittedly simplistic terms, triangles are used to describe what happens when a two-person system, under stress, brings in a third person to attempt to stabilize the system. But instead of stabilizing, it destabilizes the system because now two people are focused against one. Karpman's Drama Triangle describes the three roles, or individuals, in a system as Victim, Persecutor, and Rescuer. The victim feels unfairly treated by the Persecutor and looks for a Rescuer. There are volumes written to understand the social dynamics of triangles, so please feel free to research it more deeply if you're so inclined. For the sake of the topic of mutual accountability, I want only to make the point that the leader should never be dragged into an accountability conversation between two other people, therefore playing the Rescuer role. I know we want to, and we feel needed when we get to, and many are darn good at it. But it does not help the team achieve mutual accountability at all. So, refrain at all costs. If you must get involved, refer to the juxtaposition used by David Emerald in his book *The Power of TED - The Empowerment Dynamic*. Specifically, he suggests the Rescuer act as Coach instead. Rather than stepping in to fix the problem, provide guidance on how the two people can have the direct conversation themselves. I strongly recommend this book to all leaders.

With a strong environment of mutual accountability – authorized, enabled, and modeled by the leader – your team is poised for great success.

Measure and Celebrate Success
The fifth and final quality of high-functioning teams is to Measure and Celebrate Success. The first four qualities, when developed and exercised correctly, will produce fantastic team results. As the leader, you have two key responsibilities in this area that I want to get into very briefly.

First, the leader is ultimately responsible for execution and results in every organization, without exception. In the adage of "you get what you measure", you then as the leader have to make sure you are doing the measuring for the team. You have already set out clear goals and gained committed alignment, so now you just need to measure frequently and accurately. Communicate progress to the team routinely, providing highlights and challenges along the way, and never forget to keep the focus on the team goals and objectives. Next, for key milestones along the way as well as for achieving the end goal, stop to smell the proverbial roses! Celebrate success regularly and boldly. The only thing worse than failing as a team is succeeding and not stopping and appreciating it. Find out how your team prefers to celebrate, and, within reason and legal bounds, by all means get together and celebrate. If other teams wonder what all the fuss is about, go ahead and tell them the success story. We all work way too hard to not take the time to recognize our accomplishments. Give yourself and the team permission to have a little fun!

Wrapping up this section on teams, in my 30+ years, I've been part of great and not-so-great teams, while I admit I led some well and others not so well. When all is said and done, the main ingredient that differentiates the two is "care." If members of a team truly know and care about each other, then self-interest is low, and well-intentioned behaviors are the norm. There will always be exceptions, but in my experience, this is the key. So, start there and return often.

Section Three: The Leader and Culture

Chapter Ten
**Culture: Purpose, Climate,
and the 6 Key Markers**

We have a lot to cover in this section on The Leader and Culture and am excited to jump in with you. But first I have to say that what is going to be shared is the product of my thinking, as well as that of over a dozen other associates I've been blessed to have worked with over the years. Specifically, over the last 10 years, the team at TAG Consulting was instrumental in the development and refining of the concepts and approaches you will read. Thanks and credit goes out to Joe, Jim, Kevin, Trevor, Shane, Lauren, Dave, Chris, Jeanne, Kelly, Rich, Anne, Sandy, and Mike S.

The fun thing when working with culture is that the actual working alongside associates in the process is just as important to the development of a healthy culture as the outcomes themselves are. Even if your destination is never perfectly reached, the journey will be rewarding, so don't miss out on it. One other thing: as you dig into this work, please don't get sidetracked by what you find or learn about current culture. It is what it is, and you can't go backward. Learn from it; lean forward and keep leaning forward. I say this because I experienced it firsthand in a prior firm I co-led. We asked a small group of senior managers to lead our organization through an assessment of our culture as a way of testing some new survey instruments we were developing for our clients.

The assessment showed that our firm, like all others, had some very unhealthy elements embedded in our culture. What followed is embarrassing to admit since we were an organizational development firm that did this work for a living. But sure enough, the behaviors behind the unhealthy parts of our culture we quickly assigned to certain people; this was followed by the requisite denials and arguments by the accused parties and led to exchanges that proved nothing more than what the survey told us—that we had unhealthy elements of our culture! But we personalized and weaponized it, which, of course, only made matters worse. We eventually got ourselves on a more productive track, but boy did we prove how an organization that has some pent-up frustration can get stuck looking in the rear-view window. My hope in sharing this is that you will avoid a similar pitfall.

The ensuing chapters will line up with a four-phased process to Explore, Design, Build, and Sustain a thriving culture. But first, I want to share the 6 Key Markers, or underpinnings, of a healthy culture. These markers come from decades of experience I and my colleagues have had working with organizations and their development and effectiveness. They are as follows, and to make it easy they all begin with the letter "C":

1) **Congruence** – people are aligned with the organization's purpose
2) **Commitment** – people are fully invested in the organization's purpose
3) **Consistency** – the purpose is lived out every day, in all the organization does

4) **Connection** – people have dynamic relationships within the organization
5) **Collaboration** – people naturally seek to work with one another
6) **Creativity** – people are empowered to dream new ideas and try new things

To better articulate each of these key markers, below is what I refer to as the manifestations of each one. These references to what each key marker looks like when practiced, I believe, will be helpful for understanding them fully:

Congruence
- The organization knows what it exists to do and why that is important
- Employees at every level share and experience this purpose
- Customers and suppliers understand and experience this purpose

Commitment
- There is individual and collective resolve to contribute to the organization's purpose
- Employees show up with intentionality, energy, presence, action, and impact
- Colleagues hold each other accountable to established principles and desired behaviors

Consistency
- Purpose and principles are lived out and affirmed routinely

- Core strategies, processes, and communications are aligned with purpose
- Purpose and principles are perpetuated and sustained through changes in personnel

Connection
- Mutual care and trust are valued and fostered
- People know each other on both a personal and professional level
- Efforts are made to bring people to new and deeper levels of understanding of each other

Collaboration
- People genuinely believe they are better together
- Diversity of thought, experience, strengths, and contribution are valued and leveraged
- Working together is seen as vital to individual and organizational success

Creativity
- Inventive thinking that challenges the status quo is encouraged and valued
- Space and pace are provided for radical thinking and innovative solutions
- Creativity is honored and rewarded regularly

I hope these manifestations help bring the key markers to life. You may have noticed that the first three markers all focus on an organization's purpose. This is intentional and illustrates the importance of all organizations starting out with a crisp, clear purpose statement. Just like your personal purpose as discussed in Chapter 2 serves as your foundation as a leader, the organization's purpose is its north star, shouting loud and clear to all stakeholders what you exist to do.

The last three key markers all fall into a category I call "Climate". These refer to the type of atmosphere you desire in the workplace, and it is enabled and supported by everything from how your office space is designed to what you honor and reward. We'll talk more about that in a few minutes.

With the purpose and climate groupings of the 6 key markers, we can provide a framework to assess and prioritize the efforts in designing and building a thriving culture. The simple 2 X 2 below will serve as that framework. It will easily highlight what markers to focus on.

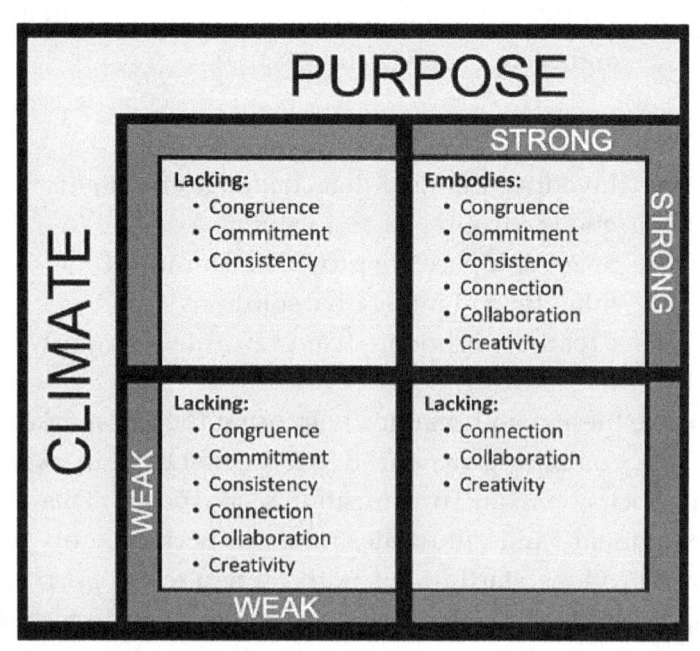

PURPOSE

	WEAK	**STRONG**
CLIMATE STRONG	**Lacking:** • Congruence • Commitment • Consistency	**Embodies:** • Congruence • Commitment • Consistency • Connection • Collaboration • Creativity
CLIMATE WEAK	**Lacking:** • Congruence • Commitment • Consistency • Connection • Collaboration • Creativity	**Lacking:** • Connection • Collaboration • Creativity

We will get into the details of creating a thriving culture in the next 4 chapters, but below are some thought starters, depending on which quadrant of the 2 x 2 you happen to fall into.

Strong Climate – Strong Purpose

If you are in one of the few organizations that fall into this box, congratulations! You have a thriving culture. But don't rest on your laurels, as there are still some recommendations for you.

- Develop your long-term sustainability plan
- Incorporate culture into new employee onboarding
- Assess and evaluate culture on an annual basis
- Perform periodic employee focus groups to identify voids/enhancements

Weak Purpose – Strong Climate

In this quadrant, organizations naturally have a healthy climate but lack clear direction in terms of purpose. An example of this type of organization is when you have a leader or leaders whose personality and behavior fosters connection, collaboration, and creativity. People like working with them and for them. But most times when the individual leaves the position, those attributes can leave with them. It's not permanent because it's not linked to a strong purpose. To improve purpose, the focus should be on the following:

- Gain clarity into the organization's purpose, and why it matters
- Develop your core principles (more on this later)

- Hire/develop employees who believe they are making a difference by contributing to the organization's purpose
- Spend time encouraging/helping employees determine their individual purposes

Strong Purpose – Weak Climate

Here we have an organization where leadership and employees are in lockstep around a clear purpose with specific principles, but the work atmosphere is way too focused on the individual. Chances are the leader or key leaders do a great job defining purpose but don't have a strong connection to the employees. Their leader's personal style might be more introverted or they may be away from the office frequently. Some areas to pursue in order to improve climate would be:
- Invest in leadership development for the leader or key leaders
- Spend time on team development, specifically utilizing the concepts in Section 2
- Highlight and reward examples of collaboration and creativity
- Assign work to pairs or teams

Weak Purpose – Weak Climate

If your organization lands here, you have a fair amount of work to do, but don't be discouraged. Most organizations with a thriving culture started here. To focus on the big items first, I suggest the following efforts:
- Gain clarity into the organization's purpose, and why it matters
- Develop your core principles

- Invest in leadership development for the leader or key leaders
- Spend time on team development, specifically utilizing the concepts in Section 2

That covers the 6 key markers of a thriving culture and gets you introduced to the framework of purpose versus climate. With that overview in place, we will move on to the steps of actually exploring, designing, building, and sustaining the culture you desire. Buckle up!

Chapter Eleven
Exploring Culture

The Exploring Culture phase should focus on discovering your organization's current culture. Like in all "change" efforts, the upfront discovery work is vital to understanding your starting point, or your baseline. This includes the good and the bad, the positives and the negatives. It will also include learning about your "legacy culture" and your "shadow culture."

Think of your legacy culture as those things left behind from previous efforts and leaders that are still embedded in your organizational ethos. They may be approaches and behaviors that served your organization well at another time but no longer do. It tends to be meaningful to some while frustrating for others. For example, I joined a 10-year-old consulting firm that up to that point had 5 consultants that were all operating independently. They developed their own business, delivered their own services, and managed their own clients. The only thing they shared was back-office accounting. As I joined the leadership and we grew over the next 10 years, the firm grew to almost 30 professionals. It required teamwork and collaboration, mutual accountability, and mutual submission at times. But we never intentionally worked against updating our culture or principles. Our purpose was strong, but now our climate was weak. The behaviors that made the original 5 consultants successful were no longer the behaviors that worked with a group of 30.

Since we didn't intentionally change things, the old legacy culture remained in place for those that created it. But it was in direct conflict with what the more recent hires needed and expected. And, quite honestly, the original consultants weren't really all that interested in changing. Despite their recognition of the need, the legacy behavior patterns were difficult to break. The legacy was one of independent, individual contributors while the current organization needed interdependent, team-oriented professionals. I hate to admit it, but the legacy culture in this case was so set in stone that we never could completely rid ourselves of it and the behaviors it sustained. So be warned—legacy culture can be very strong, and it will take a committed, intentional effort to replace that, especially since the legacy behaviors could very well be present in the leaders themselves. If the leaders are not committed to change, the organization as a whole never will transform.

Shadow culture is a little different but can be equally as strong. Shadow culture is the one you are constantly bumping into and fighting against, most times without even recognizing what it is. It can be difficult to articulate, frustrating to many, and, most importantly, standing in the way of growth. Unlike a legacy culture that was initiated by design, shadow culture tends to fill a void. It is represented by a collection of attitudes and behaviors, both individual and group, that develop over time. Many times, these are covert or secret and can run counter to values espoused. Think of a company that says they are "customer first" when in reality they focus more on maximizing the profit made from each client. It could have started because someone was rewarded for the wrong thing, made an assumption, or just misunderstood priorities. But before you know it, these behaviors take on a life of their own in the shadows. Think of Enron as a perfect example. Before the fraud and bankruptcy occurred, one of their core values was "integrity." Yes, that's right, integrity. But obviously, individuals acted opposite this value for a significant period. This is shadow culture at its very worst. The best way to address shadow culture is to bring it into the light. That means pulling the elephant into the middle of the room and discussing the undiscussable.

Assessing the current state of your organization's culture should include both a quantitative and qualitative element. The quantitative aspect will help you understand what you have or where you are at. The qualitative component will support the quantitative by teasing out the main themes and the "why" behind the "what."

I recommend using an anonymous survey instrument to capture the quantitative aspect of your exploration. You can use your own or a third party's, but the most important part is to use the same instrument on a longitudinal basis. Field the same instrument year after year to track the health of the culture and progress being made. My firm has developed a survey instrument built around the 6 key markers we discussed, providing feedback on each as well as the grouping of purpose versus climate. It is a straightforward, affordable 34 question online survey that should take each participant no longer than 20 minutes to complete. It is called the

Culture Quotient (CQ), and an example can be found on our website at jasperconsulting.org.

The primary methods I recommend you utilize for qualitative measurement are interviews and focus groups. Again, the objective of the qualitative work is to supplement the quantitative effort—looking for themes, patterns, and the once undiscussable topics. You will want to have completed the survey process and have an understanding of the key takeaways there. You are looking for places to dig deeper and places that require clarification.

To meet this objective, I strongly recommend having a third party perform the interviews and focus groups, for a couple of reasons. Most importantly, a third party is independent and unbiased. They don't have an agenda and are more likely to have people share openly with them. Secondly, conducting interviews and focus groups requires training and experience to yield the most benefit. You want someone who understands both the art and the science of the process in order to maximize the time invested. I very, very rarely would recommend that an organization attempt to do this portion of the explore work themselves.

When doing focus groups, you naturally want to group by things like time with the organization, levels within the organization, etc. The former will allow you to see if there are differences of opinions between long-tenured employees and those hired more recently. The latter is advised so that people feel comfortable sharing. Many times a junior employee will not speak up if a senior member, or person a couple of levels up, is present in the room. In addition, if it is important for you to understand the difference by location, function, age group, etc., you will want to segment those groups as well.

A focus group can run as short as an hour or last up to two hours. The facilitator will do their best to ask open-ended questions and prompt everyone in the group to respond at some point. It is important for the facilitator to be completely comfortable getting off script if the group has energy in a particular area. Talented facilitators know how to follow a group's energy and when to bring them back. For interviews, we are talking about a limited number (1 to 10) of one-on-one interviews with key leaders. You want to ask a few open-ended questions to get their perspective on culture, starting very generic topics and then gently leaning into the themes that came out of the quantitative effort. But don't be so specific that you are getting responses and defenses of what was captured. You want their honest opinions and their own perspectives.

There are a few additional elements of the qualitative effort I recommend you consider. I do these all the time as part of my qualitative assessment. First, review the digital and media assets of the organization. Do they line up with and portray the culture? Same for the physical space. Is the layout and look/feel in sync with culture? Lastly, review the latest mission, vision, strategy documents the organization created. What do they say about their culture, directly and indirectly? I have run across more than one organization where there are such simple disconnects you want to scream. For example, take the organization that espoused a fun, vibrant culture, but when you walk in their main lobby it is full of portraits of past executives in their three-piece suits. Or the company that started in a warehouse, but when they achieved sustained profitability, they built a ritzy new headquarters building that was completely out of sync with who they were. I know these seem obvious but, trust me, it happens more often than we want to admit.

When all is said and done, summarize your explored findings, take to heart what was learned, and don't try to deny or blame-shift any of it. It is what it is—the current state of your culture; legacies, shadows, and all. It's nothing more than your starting point as you set out to design the culture you really want.

Chapter Twelve
Designing Culture

I like to think of culture design as having both a strategic and a tactical component. Strategic is envisioning the type of culture you desire for the organization, starting with the culture you have as discovered in your exploring phase. The tactical side involves how you decide to move from point A to point B. We get into both below.

Strategic Design

This tends to be an exercise for the senior leadership team and/or the owners of an organization. You probably had a picture in your mind of the type of culture you wanted and were attempting to install, but the realities of the explore findings may very well have hit you like a punch in the gut. No worries. This is your chance to change that going forward and this time making it stick.

I recommend starting with as big a picture as possible; with a single concept versus trying to identify markers and traits from the get-go. Revisit your personal purpose statement and the purpose identified for the organization. Does it still fit? Does the "why" behind it still resonate? If not, spend as much time as necessary to make it so. Remember, a significant driver of how healthy your organization's culture is will be based on how clear the purpose is and how aligned the employees are to it.

Next, think of a word or two that can apply in an overarching way to what you desire the culture to reflect. Do this before trying to get into any discussion of markers or traits. Examples include terms like "customer first" and "servant leadership." I remember back in my days with PepsiCo, a theme an associate of mine was driving; one that I recall vividly to this day. The theme was servant leadership, but the way he expressed it is what resonated with me then and still does today. In the simplest and most straightforward of terms, he said, "Regardless of our function or role, all of us either serve the customer or serve the servant of the customer." And there you have one of the better descriptions of servant leadership I have heard to date. I have to give credit here to the individual. His name is Tony Sarsam, and at the time he was a sales leader in the Frito-Lay Division of PepsiCo. It won't surprise you that Tony was and continues to be not only a strong leader but a great example of servant leadership. Currently, Tony is the Chief Executive Officer at Borden Dairy Company in Dallas, Texas, where he was recently recognized by the Dallas Business Journal as one of the area's "Most Admired CEOs." Congrats, Tony, and keep up the outstanding leadership work!

This is pretty much the extent of the strategic work around culture for the senior team at this point. Going any further tends to stymie the creativity and impact the "Build Team" can have. Which brings us to Tactical Design.

Tactical Design

This step involves you, the leader, making culture a priority and empowering the organization to make it a reality. Making it a priority means it becomes a "Top 3" imperative for the organization—this year as it is designed and built, and every year after as it is carefully sustained. Once you take on culture as a priority, there is no turning back. Look at Southwest Airlines as an example. Recently I had the opportunity to meet with the leaders responsible for culture at Southwest. Do you want to guess how many FTEs they have assigned to culture? Try over 30! That is how you make culture a priority. Granted, they have thousands of employees while you may have 50 or a 100, but it's not the number that matters but the intentionality. And yes, it's everyone's responsibility to own and live the culture, but in this case it's not just about responsibility, but role.

Once you have given culture the right level of priority, the second aspect of tactical design has to do with empowerment. The key here is selecting the optimal team, space, and pace for the build phase to happen. For starters, you will want to ensure all functions are represented. Consider a mix of levels on the team. Remember to utilize individual talents as we described in Section 2. Most importantly from our section on teams, since you will participate in the build phase, you may want to refer back to the chapter that described your role as a "team member." Try your best to stay on the same side of the table as the rest of the team. With the team in place, then set expectations and provide the space and pace for the work to take place. In this regard, space refers to the time available to focus on the work. Provide more-than-adequate time for individuals and teams to work on what is now a "Top 3" priority. You can't expect something this important to get done in people's spare time. They will need dedicated time allocated to this, and you must remove other work for it to happen. How much will depend on your unique situation, but err on the side of more time rather than less. Regarding pace, this is one time I would mix in a little "boldness" while being realistic. All top imperatives have a sense of urgency and excitement, and culture-building should as well. Once set, stick to the calendar, avoiding instances where work sessions get moved or time is shifted to something considered more urgent. Always treat company culture as a top priority *should* be treated.

With the strategic and tactical design decisions made, you are ready for the all-important culture-building phase of the effort.

Chapter Thirteen
Building Culture

Now for the truly fun stuff—building culture. As the leader, you have spent time on your own purpose, self-awareness, and trust factors. You've created strong teams and functioned as an effective member of these teams. You've prioritized culture as an imperative for the organization, and you have the build team ready to go. I've seen this step done with a third-party facilitator and done internally, with both being successful. But I'm still going to recommend you bring in a trained facilitator for this uber-important step so that you don't get bogged down in issues related to legacy or shadow culture.

I'm going to assume that you have the organization's purpose crafted at this point, it's been communicated effectively, and there is alignment throughout the organization. If you need extra help or just ideas around purpose, I encourage you to look at the work of a group called The Purpose Institute at thepurposeinstitute.com. They do awesome work.

With the purpose in hand, we'll move on to the key step of building culture: the development of Organizational Principles. I am again intentionally using the term "principles" here instead of "core values." The rationale is that I believe core values are more about beliefs and can be aspirational (see Enron). Principles, in contrast, I describe as more of a "truth" that is a foundation of behavior; behaviors we can monitor and measure. We must develop something that can be evaluated objectively if it is to be an underpinning of our culture. I realize you may not agree with the distinction being made here, and you would not be alone. It runs counter to some of the greatest organizational thinkers, like Stephen Covey for example. So, let's agree not to get stuck here just because I prefer principles. If you want to go with core values, more power to you.

Building culture through principles requires two steps: development and evaluation. Let's get started with development.

Principle Development
I try to encourage organizations to develop 4 to 6 principles. On the one hand, it's hard to limit the list to just three, while, on the other hand, seven or more makes it difficult to focus on and track. Obviously, you can have success with three or seven, but again, in my experience 4 to 6 principles is the sweet spot.

Each principle should include three elements: the principle itself, the desired mindset behind each principle, and the observable behaviors associated with each one. Let's take these elements one at a time.

To make it as simple as possible, I recommend each principle be a noun and stated as a single word. If you must go to two words, keep it an adjective and a noun. But a single-word noun is cleanest and clearest. For example, words like "trust", "service", "integrity", and "courage" are typical principles. For each principle, you will want to create a one-sentence description. I am intentionally using the word description here versus a definition. Where a definition provides a very exact meaning of a word, a description refers to what that word looks like. Let's use the principle of integrity as an example. A description could be "doing the right thing regardless of who is watching." So, before moving on, I want the team to have 4 to 6 one-word nouns along with their descriptions. If you have trouble getting this process started, try asking each person to write 5 words on the board; see which ones come up the most times. Work from this list.

The second element is mindset. This typically is a short phrase that represents the attitude, or set of attitudes, behind the principle. We introduced this as part of your individual principle development in Section One. It reflects how one should think regarding a specific principle. As an example, if integrity is the principle, a mindset could be "we will be comfortable with transparency." This is what you would want your team to be thinking when engaging each other and your stakeholders. Normally a single principle will have several mindsets described, with 2 or 3 being a good target.

The third element is the observable behavior. Here we move from noun and phrase to action. The behaviors always include a verb and are expressed in a manner that can be observed and evaluated. Following our integrity example, an observable behavior could be "proactively address difficult topics and conversations." Like mindsets, each principle will normally have multiple observable behaviors, with 3 to 5 being a reasonable target.

Another way of understanding the connections across these three elements of principle development is to consider what part of the person it is rooted in. The principle itself, the noun, comes from the heart. The mindset, the phrase that expresses attitude and how we think, is about the brain. The observable behavior, our verb-based action, is a physical or emotional response.

Let's walk through one more example. The principle is "trust". One mindset phrase could be "Always assume positive intent." An observable behavior could be "Willingly entrust the things I value to the care and actions of others." The work to develop principles requires full team input and energy, and it cannot be rushed. At the same time, you shouldn't feel like the first pass at this is the final pass. You will come back and edit or tweak, and that's a good thing.

As the build team works through the development of principles, below are some questions you will want to ask of yourselves and document the responses. These will help bring greater clarity to each principle, and ensure you landed on the correct ones:

- What does success look like for this principle?
- What will happen if we fail at this principle?
- What presently stands in the way of this principle being successful?
- What questions can we ask to help evaluate the efficacy of this principle?

- What effect do we hope this principle will have on our organization?
- How will this principle enable and support our purpose?
- How do we gain committed alignment around this principle?
- How does this principle help us grow in connection with each other?
- How does this principle encourage team members to work together?
- How does this principle enable team members to think differently/creatively?

When you have completed your principle development, I encourage you to summarize your output in a comprehensive manner. Picture one page that has the name of the principle and its description in one column, mindsets in a second column, and behaviors listed in a third column. But leave a little room on the bottom for an evaluation section, which is where we go next.

Principle Evaluation

My dad used to always tell me "Mike, if something is worth doing, it's worth doing right." In this case, doing culture-building right means you also have to establish the means to assess the progress your organization is making across the principles. This is how you ensure the culture is taking root; that you are making strides towards the desired culture while identifying and eliminating any remaining legacy or shadow culture. In all honesty and sincerity, if you are not able and/or willing to commit to evaluation, don't bother developing the principles in the first place. The only thing worse than an organization that is not intentional about building a thriving culture is one that stops the process at the development phase. You don't want to be the company that creates principles that go no further than being framed and hung on the wall. You are just asking for people to look at behaviors and point out discrepancies, which is what you as the leader should be doing! Said another way, once you establish and communicate principles, they are going to be evaluated one way or another—either by leadership in a planned way or by the organization in a reactionary way. Your call.

We'll get into the when and how portion of evaluation in the Sustaining Culture chapter that follows. The focus here is simply to come up with the measuring stick you will utilize for evaluation.

In the list of questions above in the development of principles work, refer back to the one that asks, "What questions can we ask to help evaluate the efficacy of this principle?" This is where the build team starts creating the measuring stick. These are questions you will come back to routinely in order to assess how the culture-building is going.

Referring back to our example using "integrity" as our principle, look over the sample mindset and behavior to help you think about what questions could be asked. Take a few minutes, think about that, and scribble a few items down. I'll do the same.

What did you come up with? Here are a few possibilities as it pertains to what to ask ourselves about integrity.

- Are we keeping our promises?
- Are we following up and following through?
- Are we taking any shortcuts?
- Are we challenging ourselves about the right way to do things?
- Are we putting the organization and our people first?
- Are we standing up for what we believe is right?
- Are we walking the talk?

Is your list similar? Better? You will want to do this exercise with the team, generating the right set of questions and getting some commitment that they are the right ones. Once you try them out, you may want to edit and tweak, which is fine. Just make sure you are editing to ensure a better evaluation and not stepping back from an area that may be proving problematic. If you have areas like that, you will want to spend more time asking yourselves those questions rather than less. In the end, you want a handful of questions pertaining to each principle for evaluation purposes. Which brings us to the topic of Sustaining Culture.

Chapter Fourteen
Sustaining Culture

We'll cover two dimensions to sustaining culture, Ongoing Assessment and Integration. The keys in this phase are to make sure the culture you designed and built is being lived out at all levels of the organization; to ensure you are working to align this culture with strategy, structures, processes, and people.

Ongoing Assessment

In our last section, we discussed creating the evaluation questions you will want to ask in assessing whether the desired culture, through your principles, is being lived out. These questions will be utilized at the team level and across all levels of your organization. I'm talking about intact teams—groups of people who work together regularly. Referring back to our discussion of high-functioning teams, we are going to leverage the committed alignment and mutual accountability aspects of the strong teams you developed. That's why I recommend developing your teams in advance of tackling culture. You will need that strong foundation.

I recommend that once your principles are in place your teams go through the assessment process every month for the first quarter. For the remainder of year one and the following years, the goal is to stick with quarterly timing. Here is what each team is going to do. First, decide on your grading system. I like an even number of options in order to avoid the overuse of a middle choice. Try using A to F or 1 to 6. Either scale is fine, but you will need to stick with it over time. Then the team goes through two rounds of grading, with the first round potentially being the most challenging. You'll do this one principle at a time. First, have each team member grade themselves on the first principle. Go around the table asking each person to share their self-grade and the reason(s) behind it. The question to answer is, "How do I believe I am living out this principle?" Refer to the specific evaluation questions you established for each principle. There is no reference to anyone other than one's self, and the role of the rest of the team is to simply listen, asking only clarifying questions. This will require a high degree of trust for team members to be fully vulnerable and transparent. One team member will record all of the grades as you work your way around the table.

Next, start with the same person and go around the table again, this time asking each person to grade the team. The question to answer is "How do you believe we as a team are living out this principle?" Again, refer to the specific evaluation questions for the principle. Just like before, work your way around the room, capturing the grades but not engaging in dialogue at this point. Once the grading is complete, the team is ready to have dialogue around the grading. This is where self and mutual accountability will come into play. Remember to keep conversations healthy by focusing on the business, the specific situation, and the behaviors—NOT the person. Comments like "Mike never follows through on anything" are not helpful. But if someone provides a low grade to the team for a principle, it should be supported by something specific like "Mike committed to having the budget to me on

Friday, but I got it a week later and he never notified me that it was going to be late."

Two things will be achieved in these monthly/quarterly assessments. First, you will develop a longitudinal look at your culture to assess whether it is taking root and being lived out. Second, teams will naturally grow in their trust and accountability as the assessments occur. Remember, most times the impact of the journey is just as important as the outcome itself.

That is an abbreviated walk-through of the evaluation process with teams. You will want to supplement this with an annual assessment performed organization-wide. In our Exploring Culture chapter, I mentioned the importance of discovery via a survey instrument, and I referred to our survey, the Culture Quotient or CQ. Whatever instrument you choose, doing it annually is a must. The survey conducted as part of the explore phase, which provided great insight into legacy and shadow culture, will also serve as your baseline assessment. One year later, and every year after that, you will field the same survey to evaluate progress and the need for any improvements. Just like in the explore phase, I recommend you supplement the survey with a focus group so that you understand current themes and underlying issues.

But we don't stop here. Why did you want to install/improve a thriving culture in the first place? **Hopefully, you pursued culture because you knew that a thriving culture is a key ingredient to an engaged workforce; meaning team members believe**

they belong, are making meaningful contributions, and are making a difference through those contributions. And, with an engaged workforce should come improved performance. So, we don't assess culture for its own sake only, but we want to assess the impact it has on performance. To do so, line up your annual survey results with your organization's key performance measures. Hopefully, you have a short set that includes both internal and external metrics. Revenue, profit, and market share, along with customer/client satisfaction, for example. There is nothing more exciting and self-reinforcing than an organization that sees its culture improving in step with overall performance. We had a team working with a client for two years on culture and leadership, and at the end of those two years they saw dramatic improvement in culture and performance. They couldn't wait to tell people about it. It ended up being one driver of a successful transition to a completely employee-owned company; one that each employee-owner was proud of. Please do not – I repeat, do not – skip this step in your ongoing assessment.

Integration

Now that you have operationalized your culture through principle development and assessment, it's time to make sure this investment is institutionalized in all aspects of your organization. Integration means we are connecting the culture built to all aspects of your business—from strategy and structure to people and processes. Rather than introduce a new framework for this critical work, I think it would be best to leverage an existing organizational design model and incorporate our culture component into it.

The organizational design model we will reference comes from Jay Galbraith, an American organizational theorist and professor. It is called The Star Model™. Below is an illustration of his model, used by permission.

```
                    direction
                    Strategy
       skillsets/
       mindsets   People ─── Structure   power

                                          © Jay R. Galbraith
                    Rewards  Processes
                    motivation  information
```

You may be familiar with this model, as it was developed over 50 years ago and is a very popular model in the field of organizational design. I have personally utilized it many times, especially when helping clients think through restructuring challenges. The concept behind the model is that all 5 elements are controllable by management, and that all 5 are inter-related. The lines suggest alignment across the elements. Strategy is at the top because that is where you should start. Your decisions around strategy will determine the structures, processes, rewards, and people. If this is new to you or you would like to study it more in-depth, I recommend you go to Galbraith's website for starters.

The one thing I have always struggled with regarding the model is that it suggests that the definition of strategy, structure, and policies will influence behaviors and, in turn, culture. But this suggests that structure and policies are driven primarily by the strategy that is developed first. For me, culture is at the very heart of organizational design and should inform strategy, structure, processes, rewards, and people. This ensures that all elements are in alignment with culture as well as with each other. It also helps define the behaviors, or outputs, of such a model. As we discussed previously,

Diagram: Galbraith Star Model with Strategy (direction) at top, People (skillsets/mindsets) and Structure (power) in middle, Rewards (motivation) and Processes (information) at bottom, and Culture at the center. © Jay R. Galbraith

your culture principles include behaviors that can be observed and evaluated. These are the behaviors we want the model to produce very intentionally. So, the version I'm recommending would look like this:

This way, instead of structure and policies supporting and being aligned with strategy, all elements including strategy, support, and policies are aligned with culture. Remember what Peter Drucker said, "Culture eats strategy for breakfast." We need to start with, and build around, culture.

So how would integration work, using this version of the model as our guide? Let's take it one element at a time.

Strategy

As the leader, you are responsible for the direction of the organization. In doing this, you typically create strategic initiatives or imperatives to provide this direction. To support and be in alignment with culture, here are some questions you will want to ask yourself when developing the strategic initiatives:

- How does the overall strategy align with the purpose/climate of the organization?
- How does this initiative contribute to or detract from the desired culture?
- How will the outcomes perpetuate our organizational principles?
- Should any initiatives be modified?
- Should there be additional initiatives?

Force yourself to make the connections between culture and strategy. Your people will be looking for the connections, so you need to be ready to articulate how culture is being supported.

Structure

We tend to think of an organization chart when focusing on structure, and that is OK. But structure is about more than just where resources are allocated. It's also about power and where decisions get made. So, you will want to make sure that resource allocation is in alignment with culture, as well as matching decision making with the type of climate you desire. Some questions to consider in doing this include:

- How does our structure align with our principles?
- Is structure encouraging or preventing desired behaviors?
- How can our structure foster connection, collaboration, and creativity?
- What changes need to be made and when?

Beyond the organization chart, I would also encourage you to look at things like physical space as part of the structure review. Consider things like office layout and furniture, as well as working at the office vs. remotely. Be prepared to speak to how decisions around structure support the culture.

Processes

When discussing processes, I'm talking about practices, policies, and protocols. These processes can be a competitive advantage for one organization versus another, as well as critical to supporting the desired culture. Here I recommend a two-step approach that includes an audit of existing processes and the creation of new ones to support the new culture. Some things to consider as you integrate culture into processes include:

- Are there specific practices, policies, and protocols that are more in line with legacy culture than current culture?

- Are there specific practices, policies, and protocols that are contributing to shadow culture?
- How is information shared today and does it support our culture?
- How is communication experienced throughout the organization?

This area tends to be the most challenging for organizations. Digging into processes and workflow is not a simple or quick task. For a lot of companies, this is where culture can break down. For example, if you are trying to instill the spirit of collaboration but information tends to stay within the leadership group, the culture will suffer. Processes play an important role in helping deliver an organization's value proposition, while also ensuring its culture is being lived out day-by-day.

Rewards

The area of rewards includes promotions and how an organization delivers salaries, bonuses, profit sharing, stock options, etc. Ordinarily, the goal is to incent employees to deliver the strategic direction set forth. With culture at the heart of our model now, it also includes motivating people to consistently live out the principles of the organization. Questions for your consideration in this area include:

- What are the current reward practices intended to incentivize and motivate people?
- Do current reward practices support the organization's principles?

- Do current reward practices support the desired organizational climate?
- What monetary versus non-monetary rewards are/could be utilized?

Rewards are a powerful thing. Different practices will resonate more with one type of employee versus another. There will be generational differences. An employee's years of service will deem some practices more important than others. So, it's not a one-size-fits-all. This is especially true of monetary vs. non-monetary rewards. Almost every organization I've worked with has under-appreciated and under-utilized non-monetary rewards. People want to know that they are contributing and making a difference. For God's sake, tell them! Be generous with your words to recognize and encourage others. You will be surprised at how much impact it can have. Lastly, always remember that while people may come to work with your organization for pay and/or title, they will stay because of the culture. Their alignment with purpose and their appreciation for the organization's climate will determine how long they stay. Almost every time.

People

This final component of the model deals with the recruitment, selection, onboarding, training, and development of our human resources. Think of it this way: from their first interaction with your organization to their last day on the job, every employee should experience your culture clearly and consistently. To give yourself the greatest opportunity of this being a reality, consider the following questions as it pertains to your people:

- How do we communicate our culture in the recruitment process?
- How do we evaluate culture fit in the selection process?
- Do we ask questions to assess fit with our purpose and climate?
- Do new hires experience our culture in their first 100 days?
- How is culture integrated into our training and development?

I can't say enough about the importance of alignment between your culture and your approach to people. Our people are our organization. Some clients or customers will only interact with an employee or two, and to them, they represent your company. They are your company. Do everything in your power to make sure that you are selecting people that are a great fit with the culture; developing them as they grow within the organization to model the culture each and every day.

My hope is that this framework, with culture at the center, will allow you to integrate and sustain your desired culture. I mentioned in a previous chapter the example of Southwest Airlines, where they have over 30 people dedicated to nothing but sustaining their culture. Those 30-plus folks are responsible for the integration of culture into everything done at Southwest, and when you interact with any team member you will experience the impact this has. Not every organization can be

Southwest Airlines, but your goal is to figure out what your version of that looks like in your organization. You'll be thankful you did.

Epilogue: Closing Thoughts

We have covered a lot of territory in this book—your role as a leader, your role in developing strong teams, and your role in building a thriving organization culture. I whole-heartedly hope that it in some way it helps you become a better leader. That's the objective. The reason I decided to write a book on this subject is simple—at the end of the day, we all lead. It may be at work. It might be at home. Could be at church or where we volunteer. Maybe we coach a youth team. Whatever the situation, without exception, we all lead. Each and every one of us. If you agree with this premise, would you not want to ensure that as you lead you are being as effective as possible? Or turn it around and view it from a servant leadership perspective. Would you not agree that everyone deserves to be led by an effective leader? I personally believe that everyone – associates, family members, etc. – deserve to be led well. Leadership is an honor and a responsibility. The leadership you provide will influence the type of leaders others will become. Please pass along your very best.

If you recall my definition of leadership, it is the use of our social influence, our words and actions, to bring out the best in each person in order to bring out the best in our organizations. I firmly believe this. I also firmly believe that to achieve this you will need to bring out the best in yourself first and always. As leaders, this requires us to be always learning, always growing, always getting feedback, always staying committed, always putting others first, always remembering it's not really about us.

As I have pursued this journey personally, it's easy to look back and see where I was effective and where I was not. And 100% of the time that I was not at my best as a leader was when I wasn't growing, learning, and completely committed. Those organizations and teams didn't get my best, and the performance confirmed it. But I look back at other times and see a different picture—a picture of teams fully empowered and engaged, organizations performing at their peak. In those times, I was humbler, more open, and hungrier to learn and grow. The impact on others is clear as well. To this day, I have members of those teams reach out to share a story about how their own leadership was impacted by the experience. They mention how good it felt to be a part of a high-functioning team. It makes the effort all worth the while.

But it also makes me think of the teams I don't hear from, that didn't have that experience. Where my leadership was not at its best. Oh, how I wish I knew then what I know now. If there is one take-away from my mixed bag of leadership experiences, as it pertains to me being at my best, it would be to never settle with OK or good. Never assume what you did was enough. Don't rest on what was accomplished yesterday. Instead, take one additional step. Make one extra effort. Have the extra conversation. Ask the additional question. Communicate one more time, just to make sure. Demand just a little more of yourself. It will go a long way.

Please take whatever is useful from this book and personalize it. Make it yours. Create your version of it.

As we discussed early on in this book, you are uniquely made for a unique purpose. Your leadership approach should be unique as well. We don't become effective leaders by learning from others and then leading as they did. We can't all be Jack Welch, but we can be ourselves and the very best version of ourselves. Remember that what makes you unique – your strengths, your experiences, your passion, your knowledge – are the things that will help you become an effective leader. They represent your foundation. New skills and capabilities can be added on, and should be, but they don't change your foundation. Operate from this base and apply new learning and experience to it. Please don't ever compare your leadership style or abilities to those of someone else. Know who you are and determine how to lead effectively from that. Be well-defined. Each of us can lead differently, but effectively, if we want to. And never forget, Leaders Get to Go First. So get going! God bless.

References and Suggested Reading

The following books and resources directly influenced some of the writing of this book, as was noted along the way.

Emerald, David. *The Power of TED: The Empowerment Dynamic*. Bainbridge Island, WA: Polaris Publishing, 2016.

Galbraith, Jay. *The STAR Model*. Jaygalbraith.com

Karpman, Steve. *The Drama Triangle*. Karpmandramatriangle.com

Lencioni, Patrick. *The Five Dysfunctions of a Team: A Leadership Fable*. San Francisco, CA: Josey-Bass, 2002.

Osterhaus, James, Hahn, Todd, and Jurkowski, Joe. *Red Zone Blue Zone: Turning Conflict into Opportunity*. Sanger, CA: Familius LLC, 2015.

Rath, Tom. *StrengthsFinder 2.0*. New York: Gallup Press, 2007.

Sinek, Simon. *Find Your Why: A Practical Guide to Discovering Purpose for You and Your Team*. New York: Penguin Random House LLC, 2017.

About the Author

Michael Marino is the founder of JASPER Executive Coaching and Consulting. A servant leader, Michael's experience includes 16 years in corporate leadership and 18 years as a management consultant. While his corporate experience was with a Fortune 50 company in the consumer-packaged goods industry, Michael's consulting clients are of all sizes and industries. He intentionally allocates time to work specifically with nonprofit and faith-based organizations. What all his clients have in common are a growth mindset and the desire to be their best. Michael's client work, as you would imagine, is focused on leader, team, and culture development. He provides executive coaching and advising, workshops, and facilitation services—both in-person and virtually. More on Michael and his services can be found at jasperconsulting.org.

Made in the USA
Las Vegas, NV
04 March 2021